Early Entrance to College

Early Entrance to College

A Guide to Success

Michelle C. Muratori, Ph.D.

Routledge
Taylor & Francis Group

NEW YORK AND LONDON

First published 2007 by Prufrock Press Inc.

Published in 2021 by Routledge
605 Third Avenue, New York, NY 10017
2 Park Square, Milton Park, Abingdon, Oxon OX14 4RN

Routledge is an imprint of the Taylor & Francis Group, an informa business

Library of Congress Cataloging-in-Publication Data

Muratori, Michelle C., 1965–
    Early entrance to college : a guide to success / Michelle C. Muratori.
        p. cm.
    ISBN-13: 978-1-59363-199-4 (pbk.)
    ISBN-10: 1-59363-199-5 (pbk.)
    1. Universities and colleges—Admission. 2. Educational acceleration. I. Title.
    LB2351.M87 2007
    378.1'61—dc22
                            2006026121

Edited by Jennifer Robins
Cover & layout design by Marjorie Parker

At the time of this book's publication, all facts and figures cited are the most current available. All telephone numbers, addresses, and Web site URLs are accurate and active. All publications, organizations, Web sites, and other resources exist as described in the book, and all have been verified. The authors and Prufrock Press Inc., make no warranty or guarantee concerning the information and materials given out by organizations or content found at Web sites, and we are not responsible for any changes that occur after this book's publication. If you find an error, please contact Prufrock Press Inc.

ISBN 13: 978-1-59363-199-4 (pbk)
ISBN 13: 978-1-00-323474-6 (ebk)

I dedicate this book to my family—Ed, Vera, Melissa, Paul, Erik, and Connor—who has helped me to find my path in life. In memoriam of Dr. Julian C. Stanley, who changed the lives of countless individuals for the better, including mine.

Contents

Acknowledgements

This book would not have been possible without the generous contributions of early entrants, parents, early entrance program administrators, resident advisors, gifted-child experts, and heads of admissions who took the time to express their views for this project. I feel deeply indebted to the many families who were willing to share so openly about the positive and negative experiences they had with early entrance in order to help others make informed decisions.

I can't emphasize enough how helpful the administrators of several early entrance programs have been. Aside from distributing surveys to students, parents, and staff in their respective programs, they also contributed their own impressions, which are informed by many years of experience. These individuals include Drs. Nick Colangelo and Susan Assouline of the Connie Belin & Jacqueline N. Blank International Center for Gifted Education and Talent Development (Belin-Blank Center) at The University of Iowa; Susan Colgate and Dean Donald Wagner of the Advanced Academy of Georgia at the State University of West Georgia; Dean Richard J. Sinclair and Dr. Donna Fleming of the Texas Academy of Mathematics and Science at the University of North Texas; Shailindar Singh of the Clarkson School at Clarkson University; Dr. Pennelope Von Helmolt of the Resident Honors Program at the University of Southern California; Dr. Mary Marcy of Simon's Rock College; Richard Maddox of the Early Entrance Program at California State University, Los Angeles; Dr. Elizabeth Connell of the Program for the Exceptionally Gifted at Mary Baldwin College; and Lisa Whitaker of the Georgia Academy of Mathematics, Engineering, and Science at Georgia Middle College.

In addition, I am absolutely delighted and honored to include the views and insights of other leading experts in the field of gifted education. Dr. Linda Brody of Johns Hopkins University, Colleen Harsin of the Davidson Institute for Talent Development, Professor Miraca Gross of the University of New South Wales, Dr. Paula Olszewski-Kubilius of Northwestern University, and Professor Emerita Nancy Robinson of the University of Washington offered thoughtful advice and were quite generous with their remarks, for which I am very grateful.

I also appreciate the contributions of Dr. Carol Lunkenheimer, the dean of undergraduate admissions of Northwestern University, and Dr. Marilyn McGrath Lewis, the director of admissions of Harvard College. Maite Ballestero, Vice President of Programs at the Center for Excellence in Education, must also be thanked for offering her assistance and connecting me to admissions directors.

I must also thank Jennifer Robins and Joel McIntosh of Prufrock Press for editing and publishing this book. It has been a great pleasure to work with them on this project. This book would not have been possible without their assistance.

Although I have already mentioned these individuals, I want to express my heartfelt gratitude to Dr. Linda Brody, for being a fabulous supervisor and mentor and for offering me valuable feedback about the book even though she had a million other important things to do. I am overwhelmed by her generosity and patience. I was extremely fortunate to work closely with Dr. Julian Stanley, as well, and although he passed away in August 2005, I continue to feel inspired by him.

I also must thank Dr. Nick Colangelo, my doctoral advisor and mentor, for his continuous support. During my training at The University of Iowa, he and Dr. Susan Assouline carved out the opportunity for me to work with the National Academy of Arts, Sciences, and Engineering, one of the early entrance programs featured in this book. As far as mentoring goes, I feel like I have hit the jackpot!

My acknowledgements would not be complete if I failed to thank the following people: my dear friend and colleague, Dr. Laurie Croft, of the Belin-Blank Center who offered me support, encouragement, and constructive feedback throughout the process; Dr. Jerry Corey, a former professor and mentor who has encouraged me to stay focused and has inspired me to write; all of my colleagues and friends at the Center for Talented Youth and my other lifelong friends; Barbara Diehl who has been a wonderful source of support and a great sounding board; and last, but certainly not least, my family for their support and love—my parents Vera and Ed, my sister Melissa, my brother-in-law Paul, and my two nephews Erik and Connor.

1

Introduction

Describing the striking contrast between his high school and college experiences, a graduate of Simon's Rock College, a long-established liberal arts college designed exclusively for early college entrance students, eloquently recalled:

> High school was the flat, black-and-white landscape of Dorothy Gale's Kansas. Simon's Rock was the wonderful land of Oz, in color. Instead of being ashamed of my curiosity about what was going on over the rainbow, I could wear that curiosity proudly and openly. I left a culture that promoted ignorance and traded it for a culture that promoted learning. (Olszewski-Kubilius, 1998, p. 231)

Since I started working as a counselor with early college entrants attending a special program at The University of Iowa, this metaphor has been etched into my memory. It is especially meaningful to me because it seems to beautifully capture the sentiment of many highly able students who believe they have exhausted all feasible curricular options in high school and have decided to start college early. Although the sharply contrasting image conjured up in this metaphor may seem like an exaggeration, for those students whose lives have been greatly enriched by starting college either part-time or full-time at a younger-than-typical age, it simply is not.

If you are planning to read this book, you are probably *not* among those who wonder, "Why on earth would anyone choose to leave high school early?" If you are a student contemplating early entrance into college part-time or full-time, or the parent of a prospective early entrant who has become exceedingly frustrated at his or her school due to lack of challenge, it is likely that you have already developed a list of compelling reasons for considering this alternative path. Above all, you are probably aware that serious costs might be associated with remaining in a school environment that does not match the needs of a particular student. As you may know, the possibility of "turning off" when it comes to academics and abandoning once-cherished intellectual pursuits leaves some students vulnerable to serious problems, such as underachievement (leading to exclusion from selective colleges), depression, discontent, irritability, delinquency, substance abuse, and suicide (Robinson & Noble, 1992).

Even if developing any of these problems seems like a remote possibility in your case (if you are a student) or in the case of your child (if you are a parent), early college entrance may seem like a better alternative than "wasting" precious time in a school system that has nothing more to offer. In recent years, the National Commission on the High School Senior Year issued a disturbing report, pointing out that "for too many graduating seniors, the final year of high school is a 'lost opportunity' that needs to be reclaimed" (Viadero, 2001, p. 1). Most alarming was the observation by the 29-member panel that "most students, even the best, typically waste the senior year of high school by taking 'gut' classes, ditching school, cutting corners on homework, or working long hours at after-school jobs" (Viadero, p. 12). The National Commission cautioned the public that, "in today's demanding economy, no one can afford to squander one-quarter of a high school education" (Viadero, p. 12). If most students, presumably those with average to above-average abilities, are not being adequately challenged during their senior year, imagine how America's brightest students must feel about the quality of their senior year experience.

One student who entered college after completing her junior year in high school reflected on her decision to participate in the National Academy of Arts, Sciences, and Engineering (NAASE), an early college entrance program at The University of Iowa:

> I realize now that growth—mental, spiritual, and social—was the primary reason I needed to leave [high school]. . . . There were many times . . . when school bored me, and I felt like I was being held back from accomplishing what I could. I felt suffocated by my situation and was agitated that there were people who thought I belonged where I was. I lacked friends who I related with on any level beyond the superficial. I see now that this is the reason I buried myself so much in my studies. When I was accepted to NAASE . . . I looked forward to an academic environment where I could grow in knowledge and feel as if my life were moving forward as opposed to the stagnancy I had previously felt. . . . I would not trade my decision to leave high school early for anything. I grew more and learned more from overcoming obstacles in the first two months of college than I ever could have fathomed in high school. Everyone who comes to college must adjust, and the difficulties come in different areas for different people. I am thankful that I was given the opportunity to go through it when I did. I was ready for it, and I needed it. (Hoftyzer, 2001, p. 12)

Based on this student's strong endorsement of early college entrance, as well as the perspective of the Simon's Rock graduate presented earlier, you might assume the purpose of this book and my underlying agenda as its author is to persuade all underchallenged academically talented students to leave high school 1, 2, or even several years early (depending on their levels of intellectual precocity) and jumpstart their college careers. After all, why would students waste time on a "dead-end road" (as one early entrant stated), when they could spend their time more productively in an environment more conducive to learning? The solution seems so obvious, right? Not necessarily.

If decisions about early college entrance were that simple and straightforward, this book would serve no useful purpose. The truth is that, while some highly qualified students may be served best by early entrance to college on a full-time basis, it is probable that a much larger number of academically talented students will be served optimally by dual enrollment—simultaneous enrollment in high school and college. Moreover, many other highly able students will benefit from pursuing other curricular alternatives in many different combinations and for a variety of reasons. As one who staunchly believes that every student is best served by individualizing his or her educational plan in accordance with his or her unique needs, my agenda in writing this book is *not* to convert you into believing that early college entrance suits *every* bright, underchallenged high school student. Again, this is not the ideal solution for every talented student complaining of boredom. Rather, by sensitizing you to the important issues surrounding early college entrance and providing you with information about other curricular and supplemental options, I hope to empower you to make an informed and satisfying decision, whether it pertains to your life directly or to the life of your child.

If you are a teacher, principal, counselor, or gifted education coordinator who wants to learn more about early college entrance as an accelerative option for your most able students who also seem to have the social/emotional maturity to handle the demands of college at a younger-than-typical age, I invite you to read this practical guide, as well. This book is intended primarily for students and parents; however, it may be of interest to anyone who is invested in the talent development and social/emotional well-being of a student contemplating the optimal educational path to follow after exhausting his or her options in high school.

Suggestions for Using This Guide

In order to get the most out of this book, it may be helpful for you to know in advance how it is organized and how you can use it to guide your decision-making process. This guide essentially walks you through the process of deciding whether or not you want to pursue early entrance. Here is a very general outline of the contents and format of this book:

Chapters 2, 3, 4, and 5 highlight information with which you should be familiar *before* decisions about early entrance are made. The topics covered in these chapters include:

- an historical overview of early entrance and acceleration;
- alternatives to early entrance;
- concerns that parents tend to have;
- academic, social, and emotional adjustment of early entrants;
- factors that contribute to early entrants' success in college; and
- factors that hinder early entrants' success in college.

Chapters 6, 7, and 8 focus on steps that must be taken and issues that must be resolved once the decision to enter college early is made. The two major tasks highlighted in this section are:

- deciding whether to enter college on one's own or through a formal program, and
- preparing for a successful and satisfying college experience.

Chapter 9 is devoted to exploring issues and themes that are relevant to early entrants *after* they have started college. You will find:

- detailed suggestions aimed at maximizing a young entrant's success and satisfaction in college, and

- points to consider if early college entrance proves not to be the ideal path.

Chapter 10 is composed of recommendations for students contemplating early entrance, and those for parents, school guidance counselors, and teachers. Selected readings and resources are presented in an appendix following Chapter 10.

The decision-making process lasts well beyond a student's entrance into college. Most college students, whether they enter early or at the traditional time (after the completion of the senior year of high school), are faced with making many decisions that undoubtedly will impact their adjustment to college. Making good decisions and exercising sound judgment with regard to academic, social, and personal matters will help young entrants to achieve greater personal and academic success.

Like any curricular option, early entrance should be pursued only in cases in which the likelihood for success is high, After all, why would one leave high school early only to have a mediocre experience in college? It is unwise to enter college at a younger-than-typical age merely for the sake of racing through your education. Early entrance should not be thought of as a race. (I am not assuming you are thinking of it in this manner, but some people do.) A much better reason to choose this curricular option, or any other accelerative option, is that it meets your educational needs and promotes your social and emotional development, as well. As alluded to earlier by the NAASE student, academic, social, and emotional readiness for college is critical to one's success. It is my sincere hope that this book will help those who are involved in the decision-making process to determine any given student's readiness for full-time college at a younger-than-typical age and his or her readiness to tackle the challenges he or she will face once enrolled.

Special Features of This Book

If you are a parent, a prospective early entrant, or any stakeholder in this situation, consider this guide a companion as you weigh all options and make a series of very important educational decisions. Depending on your role in this process, some parts of this book may seem more relevant to you than other parts. It is designed to promote a great deal of reflection, discussion, and self-examination. To this end, specific features have been added to the book. They include:

- focus questions at the beginning of each chapter,
- descriptions of several of the most prominent early college entrance programs in the U.S.,
- advice from experts in the field of gifted education,
- advice from administrators of early entrance programs,
- advice from resident advisors who interact with early entrants,
- advice from Northwestern University's Dean of Undergraduate Admissions and from Harvard College's Director of Admissions,
- advice from early entrants who are now at different stages of their college careers and lives, and
- advice from parents of early entrants.

Author's Inspiration for Writing This Book

You might wonder what has inspired me to write a book about early college entrance. As I alluded to at the beginning of the chapter, I counseled early entrants for a few years during my graduate training at The University of Iowa and found their life stories and journeys to be so interesting that I conducted two research studies on the topic of their adjustment to college. During that time, I read extensively about the evolution of the field of gifted education and about the unparalleled contributions and accomplishments of Dr. Julian C. Stanley (who will be discussed later in the book) and his long-time colleague Dr. Linda Brody at the Center for Talented Youth (CTY) at Johns Hopkins University. When I had an opportunity to take a position at CTY to work directly with Dr. Stanley and Dr. Brody (while I was working on my dissertation), it was a dream come true for me. I never imagined I would be so fortunate to receive their mentoring and to join the staff of the Study of Exceptional Talent (SET), an outgrowth of the groundbreaking Study of Mathematically Precocious Youth (SMPY), which Dr. Stanley had launched in 1972.

The SAT is intended to be a difficult test for high school juniors and seniors but is used by CTY and other talent search centers (see appendix) as an above-grade-level test for academically talented middle school students to assess their mathematical and verbal reasoning abilities. Those who earn scores of 700 or above on the SAT-M or SAT-V before age 13 in CTY's talent search are invited to join SET, which is a longitudinal study and service-oriented program designed to support and counsel the ablest students. Students who do not test through CTY, yet meet the eligibility criterion, are able to join SET by sending in an official copy of their SAT scores. Although most students become members of SET between the age of 12 and 13, my colleagues and I know SET members who qualified for our program as young as 8 years old. As you can imagine, my job is rather humbling!

Given SET students' phenomenal intellectual gifts, they are prime candidates for running out of curricular options early. At the same time, they are at higher risk compared to moderately gifted students of experiencing uneven (or asynchronous) development. Of course, these talented young individuals do not always develop unevenly in predictable ways. Consider, for example, a 12-year-old math prodigy who not only has exhausted the high school math curriculum, but has nearly completed the college-level math coursework required of a math major at a top-level university. Despite this boy's astounding mathematical reasoning abilities, he is not quite as accelerated in other subject areas and his social maturity is at about grade 6. Fortunately, his parents have been in tune with his needs and have let him set his own pace in each subject area. They have also attended to his social and emotional needs and have made it a priority to nurture his creativity. He has many age peers to play sports with, and is reported to be a happy and self-confident boy. Compare his needs to the needs of another 12-year-old SET member whose verbal reasoning abilities are extraordinary. Her abilities seem relatively even across subject areas, and her intellectual capacity is far greater than that of her classmates, but her physical development and social skills are lagging behind her age peers. She sinks into a depression because she is beyond her peers on so many levels, yet at the same time she is not as physically or socially mature, which has left her feeling isolated and alone.

How does one assist students with such unique abilities and circumstances? My colleagues and I help these students and their concerned parents by recommending individualized programs that take into account the students' unique academic, social, and emotional needs, as well as the resources to which they have access. Some of them are well-served by accelerating their coursework in particular subject areas (even radically so, such as in the first example). Others may benefit from whole-grade acceleration or early entrance into college when the time is right. My interactions with profoundly gifted students and their families in SET have taught me that flexibility and creativity in curricular planning is paramount to their satisfaction and happiness. Extreme talents sometimes call for extreme strategies, and as my doctoral advisor and mentor Dr. Nicholas Colangelo said, "early entrance is a great option to have in our educational system. The importance and benefit of the option is not related to how many students actually take advantage of it." Relatively few students will enter college full-time before their high school classmates, however, for those who truly need the option, the experience may indeed be as powerful as leaving Kansas to enter the Land of Oz.

Philosophical Approach and Methods for Gathering Information

I would like to end this chapter by explaining how I gathered information for this book and a bit about my philosophical approach. I am a qualitative researcher at heart. I thrive on understanding a phenomenon in its context. I am also a counselor at heart (and by training). The cornerstone of the counseling process is having empathy for one's clients; that is, stepping into their shoes (figuratively speaking) and seeing the world through their eyes. The qualitative research and counseling processes are similar in that they are discovery-oriented and they seek to draw out people's unique perceptions (for different purposes, of course). As a phenomenologist, I place a premium on the perspectives of those who are actually experiencing a given situation. Thus, as I was planning to write this book and thinking about how to make the book practical and useful for the reader, it was important for me to include the perspectives of those who have had firsthand experience with early entrance. Throughout the book, you will have the opportunity to learn from the insights of students who have, for better or for worse, selected the early entrance path. As well, you will become familiar with the viewpoints of parents of early entrants, early entrance program administrators, and resident advisors/program staff who have had much experience interacting with these students. The Director of Admissions of Harvard College and the Dean of Admissions of Northwestern University also have contributed their opinions about the admission of young applicants to their institutions. My hope is that these varied perspectives will promote a fruitful conversation among you and all parties who will be affected by the decision and will help you to examine the potential pros and cons of full-time college at a younger-than-typical age.

Although my methods for obtaining information for this book were similar in some respects to ones used in qualitative research, a critical distinction must be made. Aware that privacy issues and confidentiality would preclude my gaining access to names of potential contributors, I sent questionnaires intended for students, parents, and resident advisors directly to administrators of selected early college entrance programs across the United States. I sent questionnaires to program administrators, as well. Without supervising the decisions about how and to whom to distribute the questionnaires (random sampling versus purposeful sampling), it would be inaccurate to call this a research study. For instance, some program administrators might have sent the questionnaires out to families in a random fashion while others may have selected specific families who, in their opinion, had unique stories to offer. Despite this limitation, I was delighted to receive many questionnaires (particularly from students and parents) from nine of the most prominent early entrance programs in the nation. Although I cannot say that the responses I received are representative of the views of all early entrants and their families, my aim was to draw out both the positive and negative aspects of the students' experiences, and I think that objective was achieved.

On a final note, in order to protect the privacy of contributors who generously shared their positive and negative experiences, observations, and opinions in this book, I have omitted identifying information such as names and program affiliations. The only exceptions were the gifted education experts, program administrators, and the deans and directors of admissions who agreed to be identified. All others have been assured that their views will remain anonymous.

2

Looking Back, Moving Forward: An Historical Perspective on Acceleration and Early College Entrance

Focus Questions for Students:

- Why should you and other prospective early entrants care about the history of acceleration and early college entrance?

- Based on past trends in the level of support and interest that gifted education has received, what obstacles might you encounter as you advocate for your educational needs?

- How would you describe your school's attitude toward acceleration? Who has been the most supportive at your school? Who has been the least supportive?

The Paradox

I t seems paradoxical that America prides itself on being a superpower among nations, yet has failed to properly nurture the educational needs of many of its potential future leaders. When we contemplate the ills of society and then consider how outcomes conceivably could be much better if resources were more wisely invested in education (including gifted education), we have reason to feel angry and disappointed. Some gifted education experts have even used the word *deceived* to describe what happens in classrooms across the nation when academically talented students are led to believe that acceleration will not benefit them and that they are better off staying put (Colangelo, Assouline, & Gross, 2004). Interestingly, as advanced as the nation is in so many respects, in some ways, the American educational system has taken steps backward over the past century or so. According to Brody and Stanley (1991):

> grouping students by chronological age has been a common practice in classrooms in the United States for only the last century or so. It was instituted as part of the educational reform movement designed to accommodate large numbers of immigrants in a society that was becoming increasingly industrialized. Previously, "few educators found the association of boys of 12 with young men of 20 in academies or college anomalous" (Kett, 1974, p. 11). Young students were commonly found in American colleges during our nation's early history. (p. 103)

Critics of early college entrance fear the academic, and to a greater extent, the social and emotional consequences of allowing students to move ahead of their age peers and miss out on high school activities such as the prom and other rites of passage. To some degree, this fear is grounded in reports that years ago, "social maladjustment was not adequately guarded against" (Pressey, 1949, p. 140). With the emergence of formal early entrance programs that offer students social and emotional support and other valuable resources, however, significant changes have been made to help alleviate these fears. Nevertheless, skeptics continue to oppose efforts to make early entrance a more accessible option for those who are ready. Perhaps this should come as no surprise because early college entrance has more implications than other forms of academic acceleration and, despite ample research and anecdotal evidence in support of acceleration, talented students' attempts to move at a faster pace are still met with a red light:

> America's school system keeps bright students in line by forcing them to learn in a lock-step manner with their classmates. Teachers and principals disregard students' desires to learn more—much more—than they are being taught. Instead of praise and encouragement, these students hear one word—no. When they ask for a challenge, they are held back. . . . Stay in your grade. Know your place. It's a national scandal. And the price may be the slow but steady erosion of American excellence. (Colangelo et al., 2004, p. 1)

A Call for Action: The Gifted Education Community Speaks Out

Disheartened by the implicit and explicit policies frowning upon acceleration, which has proven to be both pedagogically and cost-effective with America's brightest students, gifted education experts received a generous grant from the John Templeton Foundation to produce the Templeton National Report on Acceleration. Provocatively entitled *A Nation Deceived: How Schools Hold Back America's Brightest Students* (Colangelo et al., 2004), this two-volume report has been a staggering success in terms of public interest (visit http://www.nationdeceived.org to download a copy of the report) and definitely inspires America to say "yes" to the many different types of acceleration.

To further their efforts to support the needs of academically able students, the Templeton Foundation also has funded the development of a national research center devoted to the study of academic acceleration. Housed at

15

The University of Iowa's Belin-Blank Center, "the institute will not only initiate new research on acceleration, but will act as a national clearinghouse for information and become a partner with individuals and institutions also doing research on acceleration" (Colangelo, 2006).

Combating Anti-Intellectualism

Although we can only speculate and be hopeful about the actual impact that *A Nation Deceived* (Colangelo et al., 2004) will have over time, we must remember that attitudes, which affect policy, are difficult (but not impossible) to change. Gifted education has long been criticized as being elitist. In many schools across the nation, a student's academic achievements are not embraced and celebrated with the same level of enthusiasm as athletic accomplishments. Whereas athletic prowess is typically rewarded and highly valued, intellectual ability is often met with some degree of resistance. Those who know that academic acceleration works when an accelerative strategy is well-matched to a student's needs and is well-timed and planned naturally wonder why acceleration is not more widely embraced by educators. One reason may be that "teachers sometimes fear that accelerating a child will diminish the self-esteem of other students" (Colangelo et al., 2004, p. 9). Clearly, teachers do not have the same concerns in the arena of sports.

As stated in *A Nation Deceived* (Colangelo et al., 2004), another reason educators have not warmed up to the idea of acceleration is that "individual kids are less important than equal opportunity for all. Individual differences have been sacrificed in the political battles and culture wars about schooling" (p. 9). The authors note, however, that "when educators confuse equity with sameness, they want all students to have the same curriculum at the same time. This is a violation of equal opportunity" (p. 9). A number of other factors and faulty assumptions undergird America's widespread resistance toward acceleration and are detailed in the report.

The Swinging Pendulum: Historical Trends in Gifted Education

Combating anti-intellectualism and resistance to acceleration is an ongoing task, as indicated by the fact that government support for the gifted has fluctuated over the years. According to Lupkowski and Assouline (1992), "the gifted education movement is characterized by the swinging pendulum that highlights the extremes of any movement" (p. 2). These authors highlighted the post-Sputnik period when American policymakers and the public focused on the need to improve the quality of education for gifted children "who were seen as a valuable national resource" (p. 2). Due to this enhanced level of consciousness regarding the needs of America's brightest children, more challenging coursework in mathematics and science was incorporated into the curricula (Brody & Stanley, 1991).

Interestingly, the establishment of a National Mathematics Advisory Panel in 2006 came at a time when our nation faced serious international challenges and when the U.S. government again regarded academic achievement as vital to U.S. national security and the nation's competitiveness in the global marketplace. The following statement posted on the U.S. Department of Education Web site in 2006 easily could have been made years ago during the post-Sputnik period: "The need for action is clear. To gain an edge in the . . . global economy, America's high school graduates need solid math skills. . . . The rest of the world is 'gathering strength' and forcing us to catch up" (p. 2). Because the advisory panel's focus is on generating recommendations for the improvement of math education for *all* of America's children, only time will

17

reveal whether or not the nation's brightest students benefit from this initiative.

Trends in Early College Entrance

Interestingly, early entrance into college has been perceived as more acceptable during times of war—when the nation has a vested interest in accelerating the learning process. During World War II, for instance, the need was recognized to get young able men "into and out of college faster so that they could help in the war effort. Colleges were encouraged to accept young entrants as freshmen" (Brody & Stanley, 1991, p. 103). Prominent universities such as the University of Chicago, the University of Illinois, and The Ohio State University accepted young entrants who proved to be successful academically. Given the vacillating support and attention that academic acceleration had received historically, it is not surprising that after World War II, without the ongoing need for able men to serve in the military, interest in acceleration via early college entrance programs diminished. This was the case until "the Korean War replicated the wartime demands for men to complete their education quickly" (Brody & Stanley, p. 104). At that juncture in American history, the Ford Foundation used its Fund for the Advancement of Education to provide scholarships for young men and women under age 16.5 "to enter college at any of 12 universities for two years before entering the military" (Brody & Stanley, p. 104). This Ford Foundation experiment was important for a number of reasons. Above all, it marked the first time that the social and emotional needs of the program participants received special attention. According to Brody and Stanley:

> Most of the participating colleges instituted early admissions even after the Ford Foundation fund-

ing ended, and the College Board reported that in 1955–1956, 29 of its 169 member colleges had early admission programs. The College Board Advanced Placement Program was instituted in the 1950s as a replacement for the Early Admission Program sponsored by the Ford Foundation. (p. 104)

Despite the support provided in the late 1950s, less attention was given to gifted education during the Civil Rights movement in the 1960s (Lupkowski & Assouline, 1992). During this period, the emphasis on egalitarianism and concern about the underprivileged detracted from the gifted education movement and resulted in the elimination of most programs for the gifted (Brody & Stanley, 1991). In the decades that followed, gifted education received fluctuating support on the national level. This was evidenced by increased attention to this matter in the Marland Report (1972) and the establishment of the Federal Office of Gifted and Talented Education. Even with this national attention, programs and services for the gifted were slow to materialize. As mentioned earlier, however, the U.S. will surely continue to face formidable challenges domestically and internationally, so it seems all the more critical for an emphasis to be placed on the talent development of America's brightest students, presumably tomorrow's leaders.

The Legacy of Dr. Julian Stanley

It would be a great disservice to you and other readers to put early college entrance into an historical context without discussing the pioneering and unparalleled work of Dr. Julian C. Stanley. An accomplished educational psychologist who coauthored one of the most widely adopted and respected textbooks on experimental design (Campbell & Stanley, 1966), Stanley made a discovery in the late 1960s that prompted a mid-life career change and that literally revolutionized the field of gifted education. After experimentally using the Scholastic Aptitude Test (SAT) as an above-grade-level test to assess the extraordinary reasoning abilities of a 13-year-old boy in 1969, and a year later, another 13-year-old boy (Stanley, 2005), Stanley was inspired to launch the groundbreaking Study of Mathematically Precocious Youth (SMPY) at Johns Hopkins University in Baltimore, MD. The purpose of SMPY was to identify and serve others with exceptional reasoning abilities. The first "talent search," held in 1972, served approximately 450 talented middle school students from the Baltimore area (Stanley, 1996, 2005). Presently, Stanley's highly successful talent search model is implemented by universities throughout the United States and abroad (Lupkowski-Shoplik, Benbow, Assouline, & Brody, 2003; Tourón, 2005), serving at least 200,000 students per year in the United States alone. To date, millions of academically talented students have benefited directly and indirectly from the contributions of Stanley, who could not possibly have fathomed back in 1972 the enormous and enduring impact that his work would have.

Gifted-child specialists who are familiar with the literature on acceleration tend to think of radical acceleration as the practice that Stanley widely endorsed. In the early years of SMPY, Stanley was highly instrumental in assisting some of his prodigies (such as the two mentioned earlier) to enter Johns Hopkins University at a younger-than-typical age. He did so because there were no other workable curricular options at that time. During the past 30 years, however, educators have launched many accelerative and enriching opportunities available to highly able middle and high school students seeking academic challenges, and until the very end of his life in August 2005, Stanley strongly encouraged exceptional students to embrace these opportunities.

Years earlier, Stanley initiated and supported the development of CTY academic summer programs because he believed fervently in giving academically talented students opportunities to learn and socialize with intellectual peers. He seemed especially fond of the residential programs because they afforded students the opportunity to get a taste of independence in well-supervised settings for a limited period of time. He observed how critical these kinds of experiences were in preparing students for college.

Shortly before his death at age 87, Stanley was still meeting with and corresponding with some of the top-scoring talent search participants, advising them to take advantage of as many Advanced Placement (AP) courses as they could manage and to strive for the "cumulative educational advantage." He endorsed many of the curricular and supplemental options that will be discussed in Chapter 3 and believed that through flexible curricular planning, most talented students could remain challenged through their high school years without entering college on a full-time basis before completing their senior year.

Nevertheless, Stanley did recognize that under special circumstances, some students might be better served by entering college early full-time. In fact, he was instrumental in the planning and development of several formal early entrance programs in the United States, which provide young entrants with academic challenges, as well as nurture their social and emotional development. These programs will be highlighted in Chapter 6.

Conclusion

If historical trends of fluctuating governmental and public support for acceleration are predictive of what's to come, the gifted education community must have the stamina to continue to challenge the widely accepted belief that acceleration is a risky practice that may cause more harm than good. Early college entrance has more implications than other forms of acceleration because it involves leaving home early and gaining independence at a younger-than-typical age; thus, it may come as no surprise that early entrance tends to be viewed by the general public with even greater caution and skepticism. Concerns persist despite the fact that leaders in gifted education (several of whom have contributed to this book) have shown acceleration to be an effective educational strategy when well timed and planned (e.g., Colangelo, et al., 2004).

If you are sensitized to the long-standing issues that advocates of gifted education, as well as academically talented students and their families, have faced over the past several decades, you are better equipped to anticipate some less-than-enthusiastic reactions if you pursue full-time college at a younger-than-expected age. As you give this path serious consideration, it is important that you remain open to alternatives to early entrance before reaching your final decision. These alternative options will be discussed in Chapter 3.

3

Running Out of Options: What's a Gifted Student to Do?

Focus Questions for Students:

- In which curricular and supplemental options discussed in this chapter have you participated? How well has each one met your need for challenge?

- Could some or all of these curricular and supplemental options be modified or combined to create a unique educational plan that is tailored to your needs? If so, what would this optimally challenging program look like?

- How will you know if you are being optimally challenged? What are your expectations about how rigorous your coursework should be?

- How do you envision full-time college being different from other curricular options that are discussed in this chapter?

- Given the available resources in your community and at your school, how challenged would you be if you do not enter college on a full-time basis?

The decision to enter college early is not one that should be taken lightly. Of course, reading this book is one indication that you are taking this matter very seriously. As in reaching any consequential decision, you are going to feel better about the educational path you choose if you explore all possibilities—and perhaps even revisit options that you had already dismissed.

This chapter examines some alternatives to early college entrance. Even if your heart is set on bypassing a part of or your entire high school experience in order to enter college, try your best to look at the options with a fresh perspective.

If You Feel Ready to Move On, Why Stay Behind?

The words *staying behind* may conjure up a negative image in your mind—images of stagnancy and boredom. The truth is that staying in high school does not necessarily have to mean staying behind. A number of challenging curricular and supplemental options will be presented shortly; however, before segueing to that discussion, it may be worthwhile to consider some positive aspects of completing the 12th grade before going away to college:

- extra time to mature socially and emotionally, which could make a tremendous difference in your adjustment to and overall satisfaction with college;
- extra time to mature physically, which may have a major impact on your ability to participate in collegiate athletics;
- the possibility of having a better experience dating in college, which may be especially pertinent to males who may have more difficulty than their older counterparts in finding romantic partners;
- the opportunity to participate in the prestigious Intel competition (which is open to 12th graders only) and other high-level academic competitions;
- the opportunity to participate in certain academic summer programs, such as the prestigious Research Science Institute (RSI), that are designed for older high school students;

- the opportunity to participate in certain high school activities, such as the prom and varsity sports, and to graduate with your high school peers;
- the opportunity to address any deficits in your academic record that could preclude you from being a competitive candidate at highly selective universities; and
- extra time to participate in community service, internships, volunteer programs, and/or special projects, which may be rewarding personally and beneficial when applying to college.

Alternative Curricular Options

As you explore the possibility of postponing full-time college until you are older, you should investigate the variety of curricular options that are available to advanced high school students. Ideally, with the cooperation of your school's administration, you and your parents could develop an individualized academic program to serve your specific needs. Consider the following options.

Subject Acceleration

A common fallacy is that students must be accelerated across all subject areas to be considered gifted. Not so. While some are blessed with multiple talents and abilities (researchers and gifted education specialists refer to this as *multipotentiality*), the vast majority of academically talented students possess uneven levels of abilities across subjects. Even among the ablest students, few are equal in their mathematical and verbal reasoning skills (Brody & Blackburn, 1996). Thus, one widely used curricular option among talented students is subject acceleration, which can be implemented in a number of ways. Students can move ahead in a subject area by one, two, or even more grade levels depending on their abilities and readiness to advance. In the Study of Exceptional

25

Talent (SET) at the Center for Talented Youth (CTY) at Johns Hopkins University, for example, it is common for the participants who are profoundly gifted to report being enrolled in Advanced Placement (AP) courses when they are in 9th or 10th grade (Brody, 2005; Muratori, 2004). Upon entering SET in the seventh or eighth grade, many of the students are accelerated in math and science, yet remain with their age-mates in humanities courses. If it is logistically possible, some students who have exhausted their middle schools' math curricula leave their middle schools for part of the school day to attend courses at a nearby high school. In most cases, students must rely on their parents to chauffeur them to the different schools; however, some schools may be willing to provide transportation.

Advanced Placement Courses

Most students are familiar with Advanced Placement, a commonly used form of subject acceleration, so a detailed description of the program may seem unnecessary. Essentially, AP courses enable highly capable students to take introductory-level college coursework while still enrolled in high school. Upon completion of any given AP course, students may take an AP exam in the subject area (at present there are 34 exams), and if their scores are sufficiently high (typically 3 to 5 out of a possible 5 points), they may be awarded credit by their undergraduate institutions to use toward exemption from some core classes and upper-level placement in others. Selective universities may only accept scores of 4 or 5. By using AP scores as credit, students can either truncate their college experience and graduate in less time than it would ordinarily take to earn a bachelor's degree, or they can spend the extra time pursuing a double major, taking courses in nonmajor fields simply to gain a breadth of knowledge, or studying abroad. Every university has its own policies regarding AP credit and sets limits on the number of AP credits that can be transferred.

Because high schools vary widely in terms of the number of AP courses they offer, students who attend schools with few AP offerings clearly are at a disadvantage. If you are one of these students, you have a number of options. Assuming you cannot transfer to a school with a better selection of AP courses, but rather must make the best out of an unsatisfactory situation, you can supplement the AP courses your school offers by taking AP courses online. An increasing number of reputable and accredited organizations and talent search centers (see appendix) are now offering a good selection of these courses online. If you have the self-discipline to study for the AP exams on your own, you can even take the tests without first completing the courses; however, you should take the exams only if you feel reasonably confident that you have mastered the content. The late Dr. Julian Stanley, who, as mentioned earlier, promoted radical acceleration as a viable option for some of the ablest students in the early years of the SMPY, believed that as an increasing number of AP courses and exams became available, most academically talented students should be able to extend their high school experience by taking as many AP courses and exams as they could handle without feeling overwhelmed (e.g., Stanley & Benbow, 1982). Several hundred high schools in the United States also offer the International Baccalaureate (IB) program to their advanced students. If given the option of taking AP courses or enrolling in an IB program, students should gather as much specific information as possible about both options before reaching a decision.

Distance Education and Online Courses

Over the past few years, a burgeoning interest in using technology as an educational tool has resulted in the development of several excellent distance education programs and online courses for advanced students (see resource list in appendix). These resources may be especially useful for students who live in remote areas of the U.S. where the closest resources literally may be too far away to access; however, students have reported other valid reasons for utilizing this curricular option. Some of these courses are designed to allow students to move through the material at their own pace. If you have ever sat through a yearlong course that easily could have taken you 3 months to complete, this option may be very appealing to you. Academically talented students tend to be very active and involved in school and out-of-school activities that are time-consuming; thus, distance education courses may prove to be an ideal option for those who require a flexible time schedule.

These programs are also invaluable for students who are homeschooled and the parents who are responsible for homeschooling them. Parents who do not feel adequately prepared to teach their children advanced concepts in certain subject areas no longer have to carry the burden of teaching the material. In this respect, the homeschooling parent's role has shifted to that of educational manager/advisor. Based on my interactions with the immigrant parents of phenomenally talented SET members whose unique academic, social, and emotional needs require them to be homeschooled, I can attest to how much of a relief it is for them to know that they do not have to be responsible for teaching their children English.

Academic Summer Programs

Research and anecdotal evidence suggest that for the academically talented, there are many benefits associated with attending challenging residential academic programs (Barnett, Albert, & Brody, 2005; Brody & Mills, 2005; Olszewski-Kubilius, 2003, 2004, 2005). Aside from having an opportunity to interact with intellectual peers in rigorous courses designed to enrich or accelerate their learning, participants spend ample time socializing with each other outside of class, which often enhances their emotional well-being. Moreover, the residential component of these programs affords them the opportunity to get a taste of independence in well-supervised settings on a time-limited basis. In my view, attending residential programs prior to graduating from high school is an excellent way to prepare for the college dorm experience. These experiences provide students a glimpse of what to expect when they must function independently in college. Learning to work through homesickness, living with and possibly resolving conflicts with a roommate, taking responsibility for waking up on time and getting enough sleep, getting ready for class everyday, eating a balanced diet, and doing laundry are just a few examples of issues that are helpful to address before going away to college full-time. If you find while attending a residential program that you have difficulty setting personal boundaries with roommates, for instance, you can try to work on boundary setting *before* you start college rather than after you start. The first year of college can be stressful because it is a major life transition. Thus, the more prepared you are to take charge of your college experience, the smoother your adjustment to college will be, at least in theory.

Dual Enrollment

Just as intellectually precocious seventh or eighth graders might take a class or two at their local high school when they exhaust their middle school's course offerings, high school students who have successfully completed their school's curricula in certain subject areas often can make arrangements with a local college to enroll in its courses, assuming both the high school and college are cooperative. Dual enrollment in high school and college, which has become increasingly popular, may be an excellent option for academically talented students who want or need to remain in high school for any number of reasons, yet are ready for college in an academic sense. Many schools have formal dual credit programs, which are either "legislated by the state or have an articulated or other formal written agreement between the high school and the postsecondary institution" (Waits, Setzer, & Lewis, 2005, p. 1).

In instances in which no such program is offered, students who want to take courses part-time at a college or university must investigate in advance whether this is permitted,

29

and if so, how credit will be awarded. You might inquire whether the college credits you earn will be transferred to your college record and counted toward an undergraduate degree or whether the credits will count only toward your high school graduation requirements. If you are allowed to choose whether to apply to college as a freshman or a more advanced student, you must consider both options carefully. Although this may seem like, pardon the expression, a "no brainer," the issue is a bit more complex than meets the eye. There are valid reasons a student might opt to apply as a freshman even if he or she has accumulated an impressive number of college credits. A person in this position may envision applying to selective universities as a transfer student. If this idea has crossed your mind, you should be aware that many selective universities have limited slots for transfer students. In addition, because most scholarships are awarded to first-year college students, those who transfer as sophomores or juniors may find they are ineligible for monetary awards. If these issues are of concern to you, it would be a good idea to contact the universities you are interested in and consult with their admissions counselors regarding their policies about transfer credit. If you don't like the answer you receive, remember that freshmen may be able to have some of their credits rolled over—but only after they have been admitted.

Study Abroad

Another alternative to entering college early is to participate in a study abroad program for a semester or two. Traveling to destinations outside of the U.S. can provide students with a prime opportunity to broaden and deepen their knowledge of other cultures. Students who have an adventurous spirit and who love to travel might find study abroad to be a terrific option before leaving for college. In addition to studying a particular subject of interest, students who pursue study abroad opportunities are introduced to new ways of thinking about the world and learn about the economic, social, political, and international realities that other nations and cultures face. Many students find these experiences to have a powerful personal impact on them. Aside from promoting independence and maturity at a critical stage of development, study abroad tends to enrich students' understanding of value differences, and may play a role in increasing their awareness of their own values and cultural identities. In addition to offering classes, a number of reputable organizations sponsor programs that enable students to participate in community service projects abroad. For a list of selected study abroad programs, please refer to the appendix.

If you are intrigued by the idea of studying abroad, be sure to do your homework and learn as much as possible about the particular country of interest. It is crucial that you investigate how to prepare for the experience. Think about:

- how fluent you are in the country's native language (if you are not, you might choose a different country).
- whether you would prefer a program that assigns you to a host family or if you would rather reside with other students who are studying abroad.
- how food may be different than what you are accustomed to. If you have dietary restrictions for medical or personal reasons (e.g., if you are a vegan or vegetarian), find out how you might deal with this issue.
- bringing an ATM card, credit cards, and some currency (traveler's checks may not be accepted everywhere).
- vaccinations you will need before you go.
- getting a passport and any other documentation required to study abroad.
- safety in the region where you would like to study (find out about political tension, terrorism, and local crime).
- clothes to bring and belongings to take (this may be influenced by weather conditions).
- how you will stay in touch with family members back home (you might purchase calling cards, an international calling plan by a major carrier, or use the Internet).
- visiting the American Embassy upon arrival to let them know where you are staying, which will enable your fam-

31

ily to get more accurate information about your status in the event of an emergency.

Other Options for Learning

Academic Competitions

Although you may not receive school credit for participating in supplemental academic activities such as academic competitions, these experiences can greatly enhance your education, not to mention your social life. Math and science competitions receive a great deal of visibility; however, contests and competitions in many other subject areas are held annually, as well (Karnes & Riley, 2005; see additional resources in appendix). Whatever your strongest interests are, you may derive tremendous satisfaction from participating in competitions, through which you may sharpen your skills, meet others who share a passion for the subject, potentially develop friendships, earn scholarships or monetary awards, and even travel. Consider the following case.

Lenny Ng: A Legend in the Math Competition Community

Dr. Lenhard ("Lenny") Ng, one of SMPY's greatest former math prodigies who once was regarded as the "smartest kid in America" (Fischer, 1990, p. 1E), recently elaborated on the integral role that math competitions played in his talent development:

> It was the competitions that really introduced the fun side of math to me. Somehow tackling math problems was quite enjoyable. I was once given a photo of me at a state math contest when I was 11 or so, and I'm curled up at a desk, bent over a sheet of paper, with a goofy grin on my face. So, the main academic significance of the competitions was that they motivated me to learn more. Sometimes the

problems would be connected to areas of math that I knew nothing about, and would pique my curiosity. The competitions also contributed quite a bit to my social life . . . I still keep in touch with people I met this way. (Muratori et al., 2006, p. 317)

Lenny, now an assistant professor of mathematics at Duke University, earned an unprecedented perfect score four times on the American High School Math Exam (AHSME), two gold medals and one silver medal in the International Math Olympiad (IMO), the rare distinction of being named a Putnam Fellow throughout his undergraduate years at Harvard, and a perfect score on the Graduate Record Examination (GRE). Having earned a perfect score (800) on the SAT-M twice as a 10-year-old, which is nothing short of astounding, Lenny easily could have accelerated rapidly through his early education. Lenny used a variety of the options listed in this chapter to sustain his interest in learning, and even though he was intellectually capable of starting college as a full-time student at a very young age, his parents delayed his entry into college (full time) until he was 16 years old. According to Lenny's father, renowned physics Professor Jack Ng from the University of North Carolina,

His perfect score in the mathematics portion caught the attention of [Professor] Stanley, who quickly became his strongest advocate and a patient advisor. Together we adopted an accelerating but balanced approach for Lenny's "precollege" education. But, even with [Professor] Stanley on our side, we still had our critics, in fact from both sides. We were criticized by some for pushing Lenny too fast, and by others for holding Lenny back (purportedly to break records in mathematics competitions). Eventually Lenny and we agreed that he should go to Harvard at the age of 16. We were relieved and felt vindicated when Lenny, after one month at Harvard, thanked us for keeping him at home until then, when he was intellectually and emotionally ripe for college. And,

Harvard was indeed the right place for him, offering him the right amount of challenge and stimulation. (Muratori et al., 2006, p. 320)

Consistent with his father's point of view, Lenny also commented on his satisfaction with the educational path he took before leaving home for college:

I'm quite pleased with the level of acceleration that my parents found for me. I definitely think that I would have been much less happy if I'd had to leave my peer group. It seems to me that my parents struck a good balance between keeping me challenged and allowing me to progress as a normal kid. The only grade I skipped was the third. I believe I was getting a bit bored by the end of second grade, so the school allowed me to jump ahead. But, I think the cost of omitting further grades wouldn't have been worth the marginal benefit of taking more advanced classes, especially since I was able to take higher level classes in math and some other subjects. (Muratori et al., 2006, p. 320)

One could argue that if Lenny could find ways to be challenged during his high school years, then other gifted students should be able to generate feasible options (other than full-time college) to keep themselves challenged; however, we mustn't assume all high-ability students have equal access to resources and can make high school a workable option.

Volunteer Work/Community Involvement

Another enriching supplemental activity is volunteering in the community (the parameters you use to define the word *community* are your choice). In the geographical sense, you might define community on the basis of where you live. Typically, many local organizations welcome volunteers to help in their efforts to improve the community in a specific way. If you have a passion for animals, for example, you might be able to volunteer at your local animal shelter or even take the initiative to start a program that helps senior citizens adopt unwanted pets. If your goal is to become a physician one day, volunteering at a local hospital is a great way to learn about the field of medicine and patient care. Although you may not be given the most exciting tasks, you may gain exposure to different areas of medicine, learn what professionals actually do in practice (not just in theory), make connections with professionals who may be willing to mentor you, and experience the positive and negative aspects of working in a hospital environment. If business is your passion, you might be able to secure a volunteer position or internship at a local company. Aside from the inherent value of gaining hands-on experience, you will be building your curriculum vitae.

The word community can also be used to describe people who are committed to a shared cause on a local, regional, national, or international level. Whether your cause is political, spiritual, artistic, educational, social, or humanitarian in nature, you can take the initiative to become involved and make a difference. Drawing upon your strengths and interests, you can carve a unique niche and be a great asset to your community.

A "Smorgasbord" of Curricular Options

Depending on a number of logistical factors, including access to adequate funds and transportation, the presence or absence of appropriate local resources, and availability of time, some of the options described in this chapter may be more feasible to use than others. As the eminent Dr. Stanley surely must have thought when he coined the phrase "a smorgasbord of educationally accelerative options" (Stanley,

1979, p. 174), in order to suit individual preferences and needs, some students may choose extra helpings of one particular option while others may prefer smaller portions of a greater assortment of offerings. Using this flexible approach, it is believed that most people should leave the experience satisfied. The question remains—can any combination of these alternative options satisfy your hunger for learning or will your needs be better served by entering college as a full-time student?

Conclusion

After reflecting on whether high school has anything of value left to offer you and whether incorporating challenging supplemental opportunities into your schedule could make your high school experience sufficiently worthwhile, the option of early college entrance will hopefully appear either more attractive or less desirable. Decisions of this magnitude are often difficult to make, so information that helps you to gain more clarity must be welcomed with open arms. The next chapter focuses on parental concerns and the process of making decisions regarding early entrance to college.

Parental Concerns: Normal Anxieties or Red Flags?

Focus Questions for Students:

- If after revisiting the curricular alternatives described in the previous chapter, you still believe early entrance is the most appealing option, what rationale would you offer to those who think you should remain in high school?

- Identify the major concerns that others have about your entering college early. To what extent do you think the concerns are valid? If any of these concerns seem warranted, how might you address them?

- What concerns do you have about entering college early?

Focus Questions for Parents:

- What are your primary concerns associated with allowing your child to start college early on a full-time basis? Do any of your concerns seem similar to the ones expressed by parents in this chapter?

- How will you assess whether your concerns are normal anxieties that most parents have or red flags signaling the real potential for your child to develop serious problems in college?

- If your child enters college early and experiences the difficulties you fear, what would you do to address the problem(s)?

My Pep Talk
to the Ambivalent

First, feel free to skip this section if you make decisions easily. Having options most definitely beats the alternative. Nevertheless, the process of reaching high-stakes decisions can be stressful for people who wrestle with ambivalence. Immobilized by the fear of making the "wrong" decision, an individual might relinquish his or her power by avoiding the dreadful task of making a decision and committing to one particular course of action. A common belief is that by making a decision, one is somehow sealing his or her own (or perhaps someone else's) fate. As one early entrant stated, "If I choose this path, does it mean that I've given up another path forever?" Forfeiting options certainly is not an easy or pleasant task for many people, especially when multiple options exist, each having their unique advantages and disadvantages. But, at some point in time a decision has to be made. Have you ever heard someone make the statement, "Not making a decision *is* making a decision"? Time has a way of making decisions for us if we put off decision making for too long, and in my view, it is far more preferable to be proactive in decision making than passive and reactive. As human beings, we are responsible for the decisions we make, and because there are no guarantees in life, we sometimes risk making decisions that may prove to have negative consequences; however, our risks may pay off and open doors that set us on productive and satisfying paths. Remember that even when things don't work out ideally, we still have the opportunity to learn valuable lessons from our decisions. And, who said that all decisions must be permanent if we are unhappy with them?

My comments on decision making are not intended to convey the message that serious decisions should be taken lightly because one can easily make a U-turn and reverse the consequences of unwise choices. In some instances, that may not be feasible, so it definitely is important to gather as much information as possible before making consequential decisions. On the other hand, my comments are not intended to increase your concerns about making decisions. As one who took the circuitous route in finding my career path and achieving my goals, I can attest to the fact that there are often multiple ways to arrive at a destination. Sometimes the detours we take in life lead to growth and wisdom that we never would have anticipated and that will serve us well later in life. So, in exploring decision making, my objective is to point out that risk taking simply cannot be avoided. Once you have done your homework by exploring and weighing all options (and thereby decreasing, but not eliminating, risks), you will have to take a deep breath and choose a path.

So What Will It Be?
Door Number One, Door Number
Two, or Door Number Three?

The once-popular TV game show, *Let's Make a Deal*, had its contestants choose one of three doors; behind the doors, the prizes ranged from expensive vacations and cars to disappointing items (e.g., a crate of lemons). In a superficial sense, making decisions about education may lead you to feel like you are a contestant on such a game show: You are under a lot of pressure to make the "right" choice without the assurance of knowing what lies behind the doors to each pathway. However, life is not a game show, and your decision to open a particular door may have implications about your future choices and directions.

Fortunately, you do not have to make decisions about education blindly. In addition to reviewing the research on early entrance and using resources such as this book and the Davidson Institute for Talent Development's guidebooks on early entrance (visit http://www.ditd.org to download the guidebooks), you may benefit from learning about the experiences of other families who have made the choice to have one or more of their children enter college early. Realistically, although you may never feel 100% certain about your choice, your efforts to understand what early entrance entails and the potential issues involved should help to greatly reduce your uncertainty.

Normal Anxieties Versus Red Flags: Where Should the Line Be Drawn?

Having concerns about early college entrance does not necessarily mean that pursuing this option would be a mistake. Even parents who fully support and feel confident about their child's decision to enter college early can expect to have some concerns. The salient question is "how do parents distinguish the difference between the normal anxieties that most parents have and concerns that are indicative of the potential for their children to develop serious problems in college?" I asked this question to experts in the field of gifted education. Here is what they had to say.

It is natural for parents to feel anxiety as their children transition from each major phase of their lives into the next, and most parents suffer some degree of concern when their children enroll in college. For the parents of early entrants, the anxiety may be greater because of the students' young ages and because conscious choices were made for the students to pursue this path. It will help alleviate concern if the decision to enter college early is made carefully and deliberately, and with the student's full involvement in the process. Once the student enrolls in college, the parent should expect a period of adjustment for all concerned. Still, students should be finding a compatible peer group, doing the academic work required, remaining motivated, and being optimistic about their future. If this is not happening, and especially if there are also signs of eating or sleeping disorders or general depression, parents should seek professional help for their children.

—*Dr. Linda Brody, Director of the Study of Exceptional Talent (SET), Center for Talented Youth, Johns Hopkins University, Baltimore, MD*

It is natural for students to be a little nervous about engaging in something they haven't tried before. There is a huge "mythology" surrounding acceleration, and it's difficult for teachers, parents, and students to know what is true, what is partly true, what is mostly false, and what is just plain nonsense. Research has found that teachers hold back from accelerating gifted students because they believe that acceleration is "pushing" the child, because they fear that the child would not be accepted by her older classmates, because they believe that offering a student something that can't be offered to all is "elitist"—and many other reasons that are not borne out by research and which, quite frankly, are usually unfounded. But, some teachers do take these myths on board quite strongly, and their concerns are often passed on to gifted students and their parents.

Therefore, it is quite natural for gifted students who are contemplating acceleration to have some concerns about how they will cope with work that is considerably harder than they've been accustomed to, whether they will be accepted by the older students, and how the teacher will respond to them. Parents should not worry too much about this. Perhaps the first few weeks of the accelerated placement will be a little daunting if the student has been accustomed to "cruising" through classwork with little effort. Perhaps the new classmates will take a few days to accustom themselves to having a younger student in their class. Perhaps the teacher will be a little anxious about how the accelerant will cope with the work and how she will cope with the accelerant, but these things usually pass quite quickly. They are temporary

41

and shouldn't cause accelerants and their parents too much anxiety.

—*Professor Miraca Gross, Director, Gifted Education Research, Resource and Information Centre (GERRIC), The University of New South Wales, Sydney, Australia*

Educational options alone will not determine the future happiness, success, or general well-being of a particular child. For parents to experience a reasonable level of concern is completely normal and to be expected. Many a parent has lost some sleep while considering educational options and the potential outcomes. However, focusing on educational advocacy to the exclusion of other healthy family activities is a red flag.

—*Ms. Colleen Harsin, Director of Services, Davidson Institute for Talent Development, Reno, NV*

I think parents often have an instinct about when a concern is serious for their child. So, the first thing I would recommend is to follow your gut feeling. If you spend time worrying about an issue with your child, then seek professional advice, if for no other reason than to alleviate your anxiety. Other criteria would be something that prevents your child from sleeping or eating or going out with friends. Any issue that seriously impacts your child's normal day-to-day function for an extended period of time is something to check out with a professional (e.g., if your child starts spending a lot of time alone). Changes in behavior that are more than just mild or temporary are reasons to probe more deeply and investigate how your child is feeling. And finally, significant changes in mood, particularly sadness or even showing little affect are reasons to talk to a professional and check further into the situation.

42

—*Dr. Paula Olszewski-Kubilius, Director, Center for Talent Development, Northwestern University, Evanston, IL*

Parents need to make very sure that, even if they were the first to suggest this step to their students, that it is really on the basis of the student's own motivation for moving ahead—and, of course, the student's decision in the long run. The "right reasons" have to do with the student's being happier in an accelerated situation, that the situation is a good match, and offers an opportunity not only for advancement, but for finding compatible friends and a sense of accomplishment. The "wrong reasons" have to do with prestige in either the parents' or the student's eyes.

Once the program starts, parents need to expect that there will be temporary occasions for the student's being discouraged or feeling burdened, but if these become chronic, it's time to do something, the first thing being to confer with program personnel. Furthermore, it is almost inevitable that such bright students—who were at or above the top of almost every class in their previous school, will feel dismayed when they enter a new situation that is full of people just like themselves. Their frame of reference has changed dramatically, but even very bright kids often forget that. Parents can be very helpful in continuing to point out what a challenge their students have taken on, and assuring the students that they didn't expect them to continue to be at or above the top of this situation! Just staying within the distribution of the group demonstrates a great deal of mastery and accomplishment. Many of these students have never encountered real challenges before and now have to reorient themselves to valuing how much they are learning and changing, versus how well they are "performing."

Often, too, with these adolescents, as with any adolescents, parents have a very hard time distinguishing between ordinary moodiness that's appropriate for age, and incipient depression that is more serious. Because adolescence is the time such issues often emerge, parents shouldn't wait very long before sharing their concerns with program personnel.

—Dr. Nancy Robinson, Professor Emerita of Psychiatry and Behavioral Sciences, and cofounder of The Halbert and Nancy Robinson Center for Young Scholars, University of Washington, Seattle, WA

Before and After:
Parental Concerns
and Perceived Outcomes

The parents of young entrants from nine well-established early entrance programs and the parents of students who entered college early, independently, and without the support of a special program were asked to share the unique concerns they had prior to sending their children to college. Their concerns are stated below. These parents also were asked to comment on their child's academic, social, and emotional adjustment to college and indicate whether or not they would make the same choice today (to allow their child to start college at a younger-than-typical age) if they had to do it over again. The viewpoints expressed by the parent respondents here may not be representative of the viewpoints of all parents of young entrants, and I caution you to take that into consideration as you read the remainder of this chapter. In Chapter 5, the closely related concept of *success* in college will be explored.

Student Entered College at Age 17

Parent's concerns	Being too young and socially not fitting in, not liking the area where the university was located and wanting to come home, not being able to make friends, worrying whether she was really smart enough to handle college-level stuff and all the responsibilities.
Perception of child's academic adjustment	Incredibly well.
Perception of child's social and emotional adjustment	Great! Way better than I expected. I think I may have received one phone call [in which she] was unhappy with this stuff.

Would parent make the same decision again?	Yes. It was absolutely the best [option] for my child. I would do it again. I wish I had this available with my other two (much older) who dropped out and went to junior college.

Student Entered College at Age 17

Parent's concerns	Not enough social maturity to deal with college pace ...
Perception of child's academic adjustment	Yes, initially she adjusted well, but then chose social distractions over academic performance.
Perception of child's social and emotional adjustment	Overall, well, but enjoyed the social aspects more than studying.
Would parent make the same decision again?	I'm unsure. I think this time around, I would know what question to pose to make sure my child fully understood the upcoming challenges. But, most of all, it would be my child's choice ultimately.

Student Entered College at Age 17

Parent's concerns	We wanted to be sure he wanted to do it and not just for our convenience. He is our third child and the older two were already [in college], so he had some personal knowledge of college life and transitions. We quickly looked at other colleges ... had we planned better, we would have done more comparisons and college visits earlier (like MIT, Cornell, Cal Tech ...). We did not want him to regret skipping senior year. The wrestling and soccer were the biggest things and also a German exchange trip. We felt he was ready academically—no doubts there; but socially, it was questionable.

Perception of child's academic adjustment	Study habits were his biggest adjustment. It had all come too easily to him in high school, even the AP classes. He thought he had it under control but didn't realize the difference until after fall semester and a C in Calculus II and B's in some other classes. I don't know if there would have been any way to avoid this. During his second year in college he brought the grades up to a cumulative 3.2 GPA. He is very happy and proud of this improvement.
Perception of child's social and emotional adjustment	He joined the marching band ... this may have affected his grades but minimally. It was far to valuable socially that we encouraged him to do it knowing that he would miss the sports. ...They were beyond him and he couldn't legally do sports the first year because of the regulations and skipping high school. He has thoroughly enjoyed the band and travel, many friends, and even a girlfriend for a while. He has always been our most independent child from an early age, so moving away was no big deal. He has never gotten homesick. In fact, he hardly ever calls home. We call him usually once a week and e-mail once or twice a week.
Would parent make the same decision again?	Yes, he made the decision and he is happy with it.

Student Entered College at Age 17

Parent's concerns	Our only concern was socially. She was very shy. Academically, we knew she was more than capable of college-level work.
Perception of child's academic adjustment	Fabulously. She blossomed. She loved finally taking classes that could challenge her and loved the community of other bright kids she found through the program and through the Physics Department.

Perception of child's social and emotional adjustment	She adjusted just fine. She found a place where she felt she belonged and where she was valued for her abilities. It didn't hurt that her major was in a small department.
Would parent make the same decision again?	No doubt! It was a wonderful experience … She got a perfect score on the GRE and will be entering a top-tier university in astrophysics.

Student Entered College at Age 16.5

Parent's concerns	Basically, no parent wants [his or her] child to go off to college a year early, but when the child is bored at high school and can get straight A's while sleeping in class here, we had to let her go. Our biggest concern was having her like the geographical area.
Perception of child's academic adjustment	Very hard at first. She stated that it was "the first time at school being with other kids who wanted to learn." The schoolwork was much more demanding and time-consuming than high school. Having determination was important.
Perception of child's social and emotional adjustment	She did fine—made lots of friends, joined the rowing team, and met a boyfriend. Mom had a bit more difficult time with the adjustment—letting go of a little girl and watching her become a lady.
Would parent make the same decision again?	Yes. She had a very successful freshman year and had to work harder than she ever had to in her life. I feel that if we hadn't allowed her to do this, we may have had a 'rebellious' teenager over the past year.

Student Entered College at Age 16

Parent's concerns	Academically, I had no concerns. I was concerned, however, about the social implications such as leaving one's friends, missing out on all the senior activities like prom, yearbook, senior speech, class trip ... things the girls had planned for years and looked forward to. Our daughter had been in this school since she was 2 years old. She would leave a lot of history behind with no formal closure. And, the school did not welcome her decision to leave. They did not allow her to participate in graduation and denied her request for a diploma. Other private and public schools in our area supported students who made similar decisions.
Perception of child's academic adjustment	Our daughter adjusted 100%. She took every opportunity afforded to her. Every semester she took more than the required credits. She spent her summers studying abroad and at a nearby university. In 4 years she earned three B.A. degrees and graduated at the top of her class. During her 4 years at the college, she spoke about learning with a passion that I had not seen before. You could tell she was intellectually stimulated and working to her potential and she was happy.
Perception of child's social and emotional adjustment	Our daughter adjusted well. She made new friends. If she felt homesick for her old school, friends, or family, she never shared those feelings with us.
Would parent make the same decision again?	Yes, but this experience is not for everyone. It was, however, the best choice for our daughter.

Student Entered College at Age 16

Parent's concerns	Yes, we had some concerns [about] the freedoms allowing distractions from schoolwork and good choices. Our daughter would be leaving band and swimming programs; however, she was teetering on leaving band and was so-so regarding swimming. [Also, I was concerned about my] reaction to having my oldest daughter gone from home.
Perception of child's academic adjustment	She did very well. She was challenged and responded well. She had some panic moments, but learned from them. She actually got four 'B' grades and did not collapse. She realized that two of those B's were due to attitude and procrastination.
Perception of child's social and emotional adjustment	OK. She did not grow much, however. She was still a high school student at college. She made a good locus of friends; however, she did not grow a lot more accepting of others.
Would parent make the same decision again?	Yes—maybe. For this daughter, I would say 'probably.' I think she was happier these 2 years in the program than at high school.

Student Entered College at Age 16

Parent's concerns	That she would not experience the 'normal' high school environment and activities. Also, that we may be accelerating pressure and not just her education!
Perception of child's academic adjustment	Excellently! She is mature and disciplined.
Perception of child's social and emotional adjustment	She adjusted very well. She has made many friends who attend the program. She is very happy.
Would parent make the same decision again?	Yes! My daughter would say yes, as well!

Student Entered College at Age 16

Parent's concerns	Our only concern about sending our son to college early was how he would fare once back in a formal school setting. Would he fall back into old patterns of not doing assignments, especially after being in the unstructured world of homeschool? Would he manage his time well without parental monitoring in an academically challenging environment at such a young age?
Perception of child's academic adjustment	He got straight A's the first semester and high praise from professors. We knew then that he had the ability and discipline to handle the challenges when he was convinced of the value of making the effort.
Perception of child's social and emotional adjustment	He adjusted extremely well. I think that being away from home at this age is actually a good thing. Kids this age strive for independence and as a homeschooled student, we were a bit too close … he needed more space. He quickly found a new group of friends and even a girlfriend. I think he was happy right from the start.
Would parent make the same decision again?	Yes.

Student Entered College at Age 15

Parent's concerns	My main concern was "why would anyone want to join the working world any sooner than necessary?" combined with the idea that something would be "missed" by not going through the usual way. I didn't really have any concerns about my 15-year-old being on campus or interfacing with older students. One of the plusses of the program is the proximity to other high-school-aged kids.

Perception of child's academic adjustment	My daughter did not adjust as well as I had hoped. She still doesn't bust her butt in school, I think partly because, unlike many of her classmates, she has no clear idea of what she wants to do and where she's headed. And general education classes are ... something to be gotten through, not exciting and, in her opinion, [not] relevant. I also think it's my idea that having finally gotten more stimulating classes, she would want to achieve more ... I think the idea of overachieving is a maturity thing. Some people just take a while to realize that the more you put in the more you get out. That is one thing that perhaps would be different with an older student.
Perception of child's social and emotional adjustment	Great! She has many more friends now that she is in with people more on her wavelength, although also has kept in touch with the few close friends she had in her "previous life" (which the program encourages).
Would parent make the same decision again?	Yes, why not? It seems to be working even if she is not the stellar student we would like. How many 17-year-olds do you know that have applied on their own to spend a college semester abroad, for example?

Student Entered College at Age 15

Parent's concerns	We thought a lot about the risk that a 15-year-old could easily get overwhelmed and/or distracted at a residential college-based program; however, we felt our daughter was mature enough and intellectually quite capable of handling college-level classes....Without the support structure, we doubt if we would have had the courage to make this decision.

Perception of child's academic adjustment	Prior to entering college, our daughter performed exceedingly well in all of her subjects. She also conducted prize-winning research and competed nationally in math and science. She was fully self-reliant, took the hardest courses, and was determined to maintain her top rank in a class of [more than] 900. However, academic demands during her year in the program have challenged her a lot more than we had anticipated. Although she so far has maintained her perfect grades, she has had a few "close calls" and often struggled with self-doubt and stress.... In the program, she procrastinated early on because she didn't quite realize that college required less in-class time but far more self-study time. Perhaps too much freedom to indulge in Internet chats, social interactions, and other distractions heavily cut into her study time. As a result, she had to forgo many competitions and extracurricular activities so that she could keep up with her coursework. She could not maintain her high level of commitment and interest in research throughout the year. Of late, she has sought counseling to help her set clear priorities and develop greater focus. If she follows through and makes necessary lifestyle adjustments, we are quite confident that her college academic load will not be that daunting to her.
Perception of child's social and emotional adjustment	By and large, she has adjusted socially and emotionally just fine. She likes the independence, has easily made good friends, and enjoys the daily interaction and camaraderie with her peers. She has sought and taken on club leadership roles. If she misses home and our support, then we have not heard about it. In fact, our constant complaint is the same as a lot of other parents, which is that she doesn't communicate and keep us informed. Our communication has mostly been one way.

Would parent make the same decision again?	We are unsure only because we have to wait and see results in terms of our daughter's final academic performance, as well as her future college placements and scholarships.

Student Entered College at Age 14

Parent's concerns	When my daughter first told me about the program, I was horrified. I thought it was a terrible idea. I was appalled by the very thought of it. She wanted to go and I told her that no matter how much she begged and pleaded, it wasn't going to happen. She should drop the subject because I wanted her to be a child and not grow up so fast . . . there would be plenty of time for college. Then I heard the head of the program speak at her school and realized I had been prejudiced and dead wrong. It sounded like the perfect place for her. I came home that night telling her that I didn't think any other school would make her as happy. You could have knocked her over with a feather. This has been the singularly greatest decision I think I've made/supported my child in.
Perception of child's academic adjustment	[Adjusted] effortlessly.
Perception of child's social and emotional adjustment	It couldn't have been a smoother transition. She would have struggled more and probably endlessly at a traditional high school (even a private one).
Would parent make the same decision again?	Yes, assuming it is a program like the one she attended where there are a number of children her age so that it feels "normal" and she can have friends at an appropriate age level.

Student Entered College at Age 13 as Commuter

Parent's concerns	Yes, of course [we had concerns]. It seemed so radical. We worried about him losing his childhood, of rushing through something in his development, of missing out on the normal transitions of life. We also thought perhaps there would be holes in his education, that there wouldn't be an overall structure to his academic life.
Perception of child's academic adjustment	He adjusted very easily. The structure of college, the independence of study suited him well. His first quarter he did not get the 4.0 he expected and was a little thrown initially by the first math course. But, it was nothing terrible. He recovered quickly and he's never gotten below a 3.5 in any quarter. . . . He continues to be an excellent and conscientious student who still welcomes a challenge. . . . His total GPA is 3.75, I think.
Perception of child's social and emotional adjustment	The first quarter was rocky. My husband and I thought we made a mistake. He pouted, was withdrawn, and was very secretive. I think he believed since he was a big college student now he needed to be independent and private. He was scared and unable to admit it. Plus he was 13 and just beginning puberty. There was a lot of drastic change going on. I also think he was trying to manage a girlfriend situation that wasn't working out. But, all of this behavior only lasted for about 6 months. We had some talks about it and I went out of town to work for 2 months (one of the best things that could have happened because I got out of his way and he got to experience things without my interference or help), and I think the program director and counselors were giving him the same messages that we were giving him at home. I have to say that since that time, and to this day (2.5 years later) we have a fabulous, well-adjusted, accessible, happy, social and

Perception of child's social and emotional adjustment, continued	emotionally balanced adolescent living with us. This program was the best thing that ever happened to this boy's social and emotional life.... What we feared he would lose by going to college early turned out to be what he would find. He found his childhood and has been enriched by this unusual path. In the program, he was/is able to be who he is, to do what he does, and be respected and admired for it, not shunned, made fun of, or condemned. I don't think he's grown up too quickly either. The pace has been just right for him.
Would parent make the same decision again?	Yes, we'd allow him to do it because it must be made clear that we really didn't have a choice. It's what our child wanted. When you have a kid who is as smart as these kids are, who want this so much, it's kind of out of your hands. The children end up being much smarter than we are when it comes to their education. We had to take his lead.

Student Entered College at Age 12

Parent's concerns	Even though others in the program were young, she'd be the youngest and least experienced academically. Even though she was excellent at mastering factual information, we were worried she might not be ready for the analytical demands college would make on her. More importantly, up until she left, she had consistently used us as a support system and it felt that her being away from home would dramatically impact our ability to be available to her. We weren't sure she would get the emotional support she needed in these years of significant development and change. And, yes, we were concerned about losing control or influence on our daughter's development.

Perception of child's academic adjustment	Quite well for the most part. It was hard at first because she finally was being challenged. She actually had to work for the first time in her academic life. She had been used to straight A's with no real intellectual effort. She had to work through feeling inadequate in a subject when she didn't get perfect scores. It probably helped that we kept stressing that the grades didn't matter as much as her finding the process of learning to be rewarding.
Perception of child's social and emotional adjustment	She has made friends but has found it very difficult to fully understand the nature of many of the relationships. Being an introvert, she's found the "constant drama" in the dorm emotionally draining. She has also been exposed to many more sexual issues than we or she had anticipated. She has been easily accepted by the traditional students—many not realizing she was an early entrant—and seems to feel comfortable in most of her classes. She also has enjoyed some of the friendships formed through working on dramatic productions. Overall, our impression is that her friendships in the program are not as supportive or positive as the friends she has made through the CTY summer programs.
Would parent make the same decision again?	Yes. The advantage of using her intellectual abilities in a challenging and stimulating way still outweighs the negatives of overexposure to inappropriate things for her age. As stressful as the social environment has been, it was far worse when she was bored to depression and socially isolated.

Parents also were asked to complete the following sentence: A student should not consider entering college early on a full-time basis if he or she:

- does not have the skills, maturity, and drive to work independently and above grade level.
- doesn't want to leave his or her high school environment (in other words, this should *not* ever be the parents' deci-

sion). And, I've learned . . . that girls with steady boy-friends may want to think twice.

- is not mature enough to understand the demands of college or unable to handle the distractions, especially "social life distractions" and unable to resist peer pressure.

- is unprepared for challenges or isn't serious about education.

- isn't an independent-natured student. A child dependent on parents for homework support would be a poor candidate.

- has great difficulty with productive functioning away from parents.

- loves the school he or she is attending.

- would be happy and productive in a more conventional environment.

- enjoys the high school "life" and is adequately challenged or is at significant risk of failure (GPA less than 3.0) due to outside distractions.

- isn't passionate about learning or isn't ready for college to be his or her full-time academic *and* social focus.

- is immature and not academically able to keep up with the other college students.

- is too young and not mature emotionally.

- is just trying to get out of a situation that he or she sees as restricting.

- does not have good study habits and does not know how to set his or her priorities.

- is not emotionally and socially mature or if [he or she is] being pushed by [his or her] parents.

- does not have the maturity to be independent and responsible for his or her personal, social, and intellectual interests and is not motivated to succeed in an environment that is new and challenging.

- is insecure, lazy, not a self-motivator, or not sure if he is ready to leave home yet.

- needs continual guidance with everyday decisions.

- is emotionally immature, feels that leaving high school and friends would have a negative impact on his or her

57

life and lead to resentment, is not academically ready to assume more responsibility, is not self-directed and self-motivated, and does not have good time management skills and study skills.

- doesn't have a mind of [his] own, individual goals, a real sense of [himself] and self-esteem, individual interests, past experiences of independence, and is not totally trustworthy.
- can't be [his or her] own advocate or is too timid or immature to fend for him- or herself. . . . It takes a certain maturity and outgoingness just to navigate the "system" and the college doesn't seem to want parents doing it for them. Everything from registering, to getting to class, to buying books . . . these logistics alone can be daunting, let alone actually doing the college-level work.
- cares greatly about some traditional aspects of high school social life (e.g., organized competitive athletics, the prom, cliques).
- doesn't like doing homework and isn't mature enough to prioritize [his or her] time.
- doesn't like studying/learning or is running away from home.
- has depended on someone waking [him or her] up in the morning for school.
- has not already demonstrated the ability and willingness to be self-initiating, self-managing, and completely responsible for academic demands.
- does not personally want to do it, has not already spent a week away from his or her parents, has severe emotional problems (depression, eating disorder, alcohol or drug problems, or similar problems), and does not feel ready or capable of doing it.

58

Students were asked to complete the following sentence: A student should not consider entering college early on a full-time basis if he or she:

- does not plan to give a genuine effort or have an ambitious attitude toward what they want to do. (Entered program at age 17.)

- doesn't want challenge, interesting classes, and "real" knowledge. (Entered program at age 17.)
- still thinks that he or she is the most important person in the world. Personally, I think a good attitude is important because even if you aren't the smartest kid, you are willing to learn and have the patience to take time to learn. Of course, a student shouldn't consider entering college early if [he or she was] already struggling with grades in high school. (Entered program at age 17.)
- is unsure it is the right choice for [him or her]. With all due respect, this is not the parents' decision. It's the student's life and future after all. [He or she needs] to be sure 100% that this is the right fit for [him or her], because it's an enormous step up from being pampered at home and in high school. I knew from the first day of high school that I wanted to enter college early and I've never looked back even for a second. I've seen people doubt themselves and their motives and then fall through the cracks. It's tough going to college early and it's most certainly not for everyone. (Entered program at age 16.)
- is not ready for adult responsibilities. (Entered program at age 16.)
- is loyal to family and friends to the extreme, is emotionally attached to high school, and his or her grades aren't up to par. (Entered program at age 16.)
- depends on his mom to wake him up each day, to wash his clothes, make him study, or go to soccer practice; if she is more interested in making friends than making the grade; is very attached to his parents and can hardly go a day without missing them; is sufficiently challenged and satisfied at her current school. (Entered program at age 15.)
- does not know how to manage [his or her] time. (Entered program at age 15.)
- thinks of the program as a purely social experience. [Although] the social aspect of early college admission is important, academics must also be given priority. Students shouldn't go to college simply to avoid their parents or to have fun. One must be open to learning

new things and making new friends. (Entered program at age 15.)

- isn't excited about it. There's no reason to do it if you don't want to, if you aren't eager to move on. (Entered college on his own at age 14.)
- is not driven and motivated. I've seen talented and smart people flunk out because they're unwilling to put in the work. Many others languish and could do much better if they were willing to spend more effort and time. To put it another way, if you don't have a love of learning, college is probably not for you and a waste of time and money. (Entered program at age 13.)
- is immature and is unwilling to do the work. (Entered program at age 13.)

Conclusion

In this chapter, experts on gifted education, parents, and early entrants shared their insights and experiences in order to assist readers in the decision-making process. Cognizant that parents are faced with the difficult task of distinguishing between normal anxieties and warning signs of serious problems, leaders in gifted education offered their advice to parents. One general conclusion is that while it is unrealistic for parents to expect their children to have problem-free adjustments to college, they must also be able to determine when it is unrealistic to expect their children to adapt well, for example, when these individuals lack the internal resources (or are not ready) to function independently. Parents must be mindful of whose motivation is driving the decision for their children to follow particular paths. In each instance, a parent must assess whether it is his or her own desire or the child's wish to move on to college earlier than expected. Trusting their own instincts, parents should not hesitate to seek professional consultation if concerns regarding their children persist. Mental health and emotional issues such as depression and anxiety are treatable; thus, it would be a shame for a student afflicted with a serious issue to suffer through the college experience because of an undiagnosed and untreated problem.

As we learned from the parent contributors, their concerns did not inevitably lead to the worst-case scenarios that may have been lurking in the back of their minds. In fact, many parents were pleasantly surprised that their children adjusted as well as they did. In some cases, parents' concerns were warranted to an extent, but for the most part, the students adjusted to college rather well—even those who experienced minor setbacks. By commenting on the conditions under which a student should not enter college early, student and parent contributors provided even more information to factor into the decision-making process. If you have found the contributors' comments to be helpful, you will not want to miss Chapter 5, which continues the discussion on college adjustment by examining factors that both promote and hinder success in college.

5

Why Some Early Entrants Thrive in College and Others Don't

Focus Questions for Students:

- How do you define *success* for yourself?
- How do significant others in your life define *success*?
- What personal qualities/characteristics do you recognize in yourself that may help and/or hinder your adjustment to college?
- What feedback have you received from others (e.g., family members, friends, teachers) regarding your personal qualities/characteristics that may help and/or hinder your adjustment to college?
- What environmental factors may influence your adjustment to college in both positive and negative ways?
- What do you need from others in order to achieve success (as you define it)? Be specific.

Focus Questions for Parents:

- How do you define *success* for your child?
- What personal qualities/characteristics does your child possess that may help and/or hinder his or her adjustment to college?
- What external or environmental factors may help and/or hinder your child in college?

Questioning My Own Success

Every Ph.D. candidate has his or her dissertation nightmares. Some happen in one's dreams (like forgetting to show up at one's defense: "Gosh, wasn't there something I was supposed to do today?"), whereas others happen in one's waking hours. During the final stage of preparing my dissertation manuscript, I felt a growing sense of uneasiness, which by the day before my defense had become full-blown panic. I was afraid that my committee would ask a fundamental question that I would not be able to answer. My research focused on the academic, social, and emotional adjustment of a cohort of early entrants. Surely my committee would ask me to discuss whether or not these students were successful in their experience. After transcribing and analyzing more than 800 pages of data (single-spaced, might I add) and then writing a 525-page dissertation, I was uncertain as to how I would answer that question. I delved into the lives of 10 students, spent countless hours and reams of paper (and I mean reams!), and even dreamed about this project—and could not define the seemingly straightforward concept of success. Somehow, I didn't think the words "I don't know" would impress my professors. Fortunately, I "successfully" completed my defense and was relieved to know that my lack of a firm conclusion was not the result of "dissertation dementia" (the deterioration of one's cognitive functioning during the dissertation process, in case you are interested), but rather, was the result of probing deeply into my subject and seeing the concept or construct of success in a much more complex and multifaceted manner.

In the years that have passed since I earned my doctorate, I must admit that I still find the concept of success for early entrants difficult to define. Should success be determined by a student's level of satisfaction with his or her decision to enter college early and his or her college experiences, or should academic success (e.g., GPA) be the main criterion? And, what about happiness? How does that fit into the equation? Are satisfaction and happiness inextricably related, or is the relationship not always predictable? Should success or lack thereof be determined by how well a student fares in a particular early entrance program (e.g., if he or she remains in a program or leaves a program prematurely), and if so, is that a reflection of the student's success or failure, the program's success or failure, a combination of both, or none of the above? To complicate matters even more, because early entrance programs have their unique features and goals, it does not seem reasonable or fair to identify only one standard of success—and perhaps the students who opt to enter college on their own (without the support of a special program) use different criteria to assess their success. Finally, we must not forget that cultural factors color people's perceptions about what constitutes success. My point in posing these questions is to illustrate that offering a single definition of or standard for success (in college) may not be useful or even appropriate. An important first step is to reflect on the meaning of success. What do you believe is the best way to define and measure success?

Early Entrants' Perceptions of Success

The student respondents shared their definitions of success and commented on whether or not they perceived they had achieved success in college. Here are some of their responses:

> Success has always been defined by getting good grades and in that respect, I didn't get off to a great start, but I'm doing better there. Socially, I've been pretty successful with the help of joining the marching band here. (Entered program at age 17.)

Success, to me, means achieving your expectations. . . .
Overall, yes, [I have achieved success] because I worked
very hard. (Entered program at age 17.)

Before coming to college, success meant earning lots of
money and being better than everyone else. After spending 2 years at college, I am convinced that it's impossible
to know everything. . . . There are a lot of people who are
experts in many different areas. Also, I've come to realize
that you can't live your life by yourself on an island. There
needs to be a community of friends. So, with all of that in
mind, I think success is to be excellent in all that I do and
willing to look out for those around me. It's not how much
I gain that determines my success, but how much I can contribute. Yes, I believe I have achieved success. Well, at least I'm
working towards it. (Entered program at age 17.)

Success is achieving personal standards that one has set for
him- or herself. Although I haven't maintained my 4.0, I come
close. I think I have been very successful. After all, I am 2
years ahead of the game. (Entered program at age 16.)

Success is doing well to the best of one's abilities despite
setbacks and/or failures. Although I feel I could have done
better in certain classes or situations, I truly believe I have
achieved some success, but that doesn't mean I am going to
stop. (Entered program at age 16.)

Most of the students I knew in the program were fleeing
something or someone at least as much as looking to succeed.
Personally, I was looking to be intellectually challenged—or
at least not bored—by my courses and not to spend a year
in high school waiting to go to college. I'm not sure I would
refer to these goals with the word success, but if you choose
to then I was successful. (Entered program at age 16.)

I do not feel that this question about success is really possible
to answer at age 18, as I have yet to reap the fruits of my work,
whatever they may be. In 30 years, I might, but even then
one might say that there are any number of paths to a goal.

Certainly, I feel I have learned and grown much more than my friends who are now only finishing high school. In that sense, I feel my time here has been a success. . . . In a non-academic sense, living away from my parents for 2 years has been enormously freeing. I get more sleep at college (a cool 9 hours a night) than I ever did in high school. (Entered program at age 16.)

I believe success . . . is making the right choice for you and being happy with that decision. Without boasting, I think I am successful and the program helped me to get there. I knew high school didn't have the opportunities I yearned for. I am successful in that I came here, took absolute advantage of everything the university offered, and I excelled. In 2 years, I have a math minor, I'm less than a handful of courses away from a math major, I did neuroscience research with a professor/mentor, and I'm going to Cal Tech next year. The program afforded me all of these steps to success and I'm very thankful for it. (Entered program at age 16.)

Learning new things (started rock climbing and karate), being academically and culturally challenged, taking advantage of a stimulating environment, getting good grades, doing a few "extra" things (signed up for independent study in nursing, was elected treasurer for nursing student organization, had a part-time job, attended events). Yes, I have achieved success! (Entered program at age 15.)

I think success . . . is more than just excelling in classes. While grades are very important . . . success means much more than that. [Attending] this program means being one of the best and being able to balance all aspects of [student life]. We ought to be leaders, setting examples for others. . . . I have become a club leader and still was able to maintain decent grades while helping others and making the best of the experience. (Entered program at age 15.)

I believe that I definitely succeeded. I have had 2+ years of research experience. . . . I am not worried about acceptance

> to grad school for my Ph.D. I am confident. I have learned my subject well. (Entered program at age 14.)

> I have a high GPA and will be going to medical school. I have a large circle of friends, am excited about going to school, and am happy and content after 5 years. (Entered program at age 14.)

> A successful college education means to me: learning the skill sets for my career, developing a social network, growing personally, and enjoying it. Overall, yes, I think I have achieved some measure of success. (Entered program at age 13.)

Although these students measured success partially on the basis of their academic performance in college, a number of them alluded to the importance of social and emotional growth. Consistent with research on early entrance (e.g., Olszewski-Kubilius, 1995), the students who contributed to this book considered themselves successful for the most part; however, a few students did not regard their overall college experience a success. For instance, one former student who entered college at age 15 after graduating from high school stated, "I did not succeed. I graduated from a different college than I wanted, in a different major, with few friends, and a GPA too bad to put on a job application." Although this young woman admitted that her life turned around after college and that her life certainly was "not a failure," as she had established a full-time career in the entertainment industry, she did acknowledge that it was "debatable" whether she needed "to go to college at all." She pointed out, "If I'd spent the same amount of money and time working on independent films I'd probably be much better off."

Another student who entered college one year early through a formal program left after one semester and returned to high school. She did not feel successful as an early entrant and recognized that she needed the extra year to bring closure to her high school experience. Instead of feeling like part of a community, she perceived "the distinction of being in the program as not so helpful because it sort of set me apart. I felt

I wasn't really a part of the whole college community." Due to a conflict with her roommate, this student transferred to a new residence hall and hoped to establish new friendships there. Although she met new people, they were older, and as she put it, "that made me feel like I was even younger. It made me feel like I really didn't belong there . . . like I should be back in high school because I was just a kid." She acknowledged that her brief early entrance experience "indirectly caused hardship" in her personal life. This example underscores how critical it is for a student to be ready for the social and emotional adjustment to college life.

Parents' Perceptions of Early Entrants' Success

Parents of early entrants also offered their definitions of success and appraised how well their children fared in college. Most of the respondents viewed their children as successful in at least some respects and defined success on the basis of academic, social, and emotional adjustment:

> Our daughter has grown much more than she would have had she stayed "in the nest" for another academic year. To us, success means that she has grown in her insights of self and the world and has gained confidence in her abilities and talents, not to mention maintained a high scholastic standing (all A's).

> My daughter has not achieved as much success as I would have hoped academically, but if success is measured by growth, maturity, and contentment, then yes, she is successful. She is learning, if nothing else, how to deal in the adult world, and what she can or has to do to get where she wants.

69

> One kind of success will be graduation, plain and simple . . .

Our daughter has great confidence in herself. Her esteem increases as she progresses. That is success, with a bonus of an outstanding education.

My child has achieved success by proving to herself that being "different" is okay. She is excelling academically and is well-adjusted socially. She is happy where she is.

We wanted our son to learn, of course, to be able to move forward academically at a challenging pace, but mostly we wanted him to thrive socially and emotionally. So yes. Definitely. He's a confident, independent, funny, happy teenager.

Success is attending classes, completing assignments, working well with other students, using faculty feedback productively, and maintaining at least a B average in all classes. Also, discovering and pursuing her passions/interests, being excited about what she's learning in some of her classes, and accepting that some classes are requirements to be done responsibly if not with incredible enthusiasm.

Success meant successfully adjusting to new living situations, good grades, his report that classes were intriguing and challenging, having friends, staying focused on school, making his way doing the business and tasks that are occasionally required—responsibly and timely. Yes, he has succeeded greatly.

We wanted her to have academic challenges and to learn a lot about her chosen field. We also expected good grades based on her high school performance and abilities. . . . Her GPA of 3.75 could have been higher given her ability level, but we supported her decisions to make time for other activities by not obsessing about straight A's.

Success in this context would be happiness and fulfillment. She was successful both academically and socially. She conquered her demons in her math courses. She took a breadth and depth of courses she would not have been able to take at her home high school. She was happy to be in an environment where the challenge to achieve was intense and where the students engaged that challenge intensely. On the negative side, she compared herself to the math minds around her, and found herself lacking. She decided that she should choose a life profession in another area than math or hard science.

Academically, she tackled the courses, added additional courses, filled her hours and her brain. She was happy because she felt she was able to learn as much as she could fit into her waking time. She was also successful in a way I hadn't anticipated—she learned her limits. Her third semester, she was taking 23 hours plus auditing two 3-hour courses. She did not have time to manage all of the work so [she] had to drop one of the courses she was auditing. Also, her grade in one course was a B so her average dropped below a 4.0. This was thrilling to me because for the first time she was learning that she had limits in what she could manage to accomplish in her time. That is a valuable lesson in life. Socially, she was happy because she was communicating with peers. She was happy to be competing with other agile minds. She was thrilled to find minds more able than her own.

One critical point to remember is that college students, whether they enter early or at the traditional time, do not simply divorce themselves from their emotional issues or struggles when they leave for college. College success and adjustment are likely to be influenced by unresolved issues that students bring with them. For instance, when asked about her daughter's adjustment to college, one parent described a tragic event that occurred shortly before her daughter left for college at age 15:

She experienced the suicide of a young man from her high school whom she had very much admired—and she became seriously depressed over the summer. Our concerns [in her leaving for college] were less related to college academics, but rather her emotional state—wherever she was. She had always demonstrated maturity and an ability to interact ably with anyone regardless of age, but we discovered that she had also begun "cutting" as a coping mechanism. We were hoping that a new setting with more advanced peers and challenging faculty members—in a small supportive liberal arts setting—as well as ongoing counseling—could help her through this dangerous period . . .

This student eventually did seriously harm herself during her sophomore year in college by taking an overdose of over-the-counter medication and ended up in intensive care; however, she did survive. Her mother suggested that despite the difficult adjustment she made, she was still able to accomplish her academic goals:

> . . . but most importantly, she survived a major depressive episode and quit self-mutilating behaviors. She envisioned a future for herself that included travel, and an MFA in translation and she pursued those goals. She had friends. She had experiences that she valued, including a trip for highly able "high school students" to DC (since she had no high school diploma, she was still eligible for these things—one advantage to NOT being awarded a diploma early!). We never defined success as a certain major or GPA. For our daughter, it was [finding] a setting that could help her find her way emotionally, without penalizing her for her intellectual prowess.

In another instance, a parent pointed out that her daughter's asynchronous development may have been detrimental to her success as an early entrant. Although she was academically capable of mastering college coursework, her mother reported that "the maturity wasn't there" and that she "didn't adjust very well." This student's father shared his opinion that his daughter's adjustment to college "was really hard . . .

extremely hard." He did not believe that "she knew what she was in for" and added, "the first roommate made it really, really hard for her. I think she was lonely and scared and then the problem with the roommate came up. It just all added up and it was too much." Although this young woman left college after a semester and returned to high school to graduate with her high school peers, she reentered college the next school year at a major university that was much closer to home and felt prepared for the experience her second time around. Her subsequent college experience was much more positive and she claimed to be much happier academically, socially, and otherwise.

Factors That Contribute to and Detract From Early Entrants' Success in College

Because success can be assessed along various dimensions, it would be simplistic to dichotomize a student as either "successful" or "unsuccessful." Even those who have failed academically have positive qualities that may have contributed to the positive aspects of their experience. Conversely, even students who have proven themselves to be academic superstars may possess qualities that detracted from their success socially or emotionally. In order to better understand the personal qualities and external factors (e.g., level of support from family, friendships) that may contribute to and hinder success, the student and parent respondents shared their perceptions of the factors that made a difference in both positive and negative ways.

Student Perspectives About Factors That Promote Success

My own research on the adjustment of early entrance students indicated that the most academically successful ones were those who could be described as "focused, goal-oriented, perseverant, driven, self-disciplined, and/or hard working (or as having a strong work ethic)" (Muratori, 2003, p. 395). Additionally, family support appeared to be a critical factor for them. Other helpful influences were supportive peers and friends, as well as program staff (Muratori, 2003). The students who responded to the questionnaire for this book added their comments about factors that have been helpful to them. A few of their responses are listed below.

My parents are not here next to me telling me what to do [and] it forces me to become a more mature, responsible person. And, with that maturity, I learn about life . . . and to live that life to the fullest. . . . My hall director has been an inspiration to me these past 2 years. Not only does she encourage me to be intentional with my time, but she also challenges me to live this life significantly. (Entered program at age 17.)

I'd like to think talent has carried me this far, but I'm no genius so that's probably not it. I think a focus and maturity that my classmates lacked has helped me to succeed. Some people work extremely hard to get into a great college, and when they get in, they think the battle has been won. For me, the battle never ended. I went from college prep mode to graduate prep mode. Everyone was very cordial and friendly . . . I never felt pressured or intimidated or alone, and I think that helped me adapt to my new environment as quickly as I did. . . . My parents were supportive too; they never questioned my decision. (Entered program at age 17.)

Time management—essential; parental support (calls, e-mails, and food always helped); maturity (many people think I am "old" for my age); mentoring by students and adults (staff, counselors, etc.); motivation to eventually support my family;

determination to do well; patience (everything takes time, often more than you seem to have); and good organization, which saves so much time in the end. (Entered program at age 16.)

I was always very independent. Being able to do things on my own without looking to the crowd for encouragement has made me strong. I'm good at time management, which is absolutely critical in college. I've also had a few out-of-this-world phenomenal mentors along the way . . . [who] pushed me to expand my capabilities. I've also had some fantastic professors . . . (Entered program at age 16.)

Both in my academics and sports career, I have achieved success through motivation and an almost unhealthy single-mindedness in my ability to focus. My parents were of great help in teaching me . . . the value of hard work and the reading and over-the-top school projects that my father thrust on me, although incredibly aggravating at the time, have definitely been of use to me now that I am more or less an adult. (Entered program at age 16.)

Support from my parents was definitely critical. Mom proofread nearly all of my papers (which I would e-mail her). I hate to have to mention it, but without my parents' and grandparents' financial support, I also wouldn't have been able to attend the program. My parents also provided emotional support. . . . Understanding and sympathetic faculty members were also crucial to my ability to succeed. . . . I'm able to work intensely for short periods of time and that was the only way I could succeed academically. (Entered program at age 16.)

My seventh-grade math teacher once described me as a 35-year-old CEO trapped in an eighth grader's body, so my maturity has definitely contributed to my success since many of my other traits stem from it. I am independent, self-motivated, and organized. Above all, I manage my time well and I do not procrastinate . . . (Entered program at age 16.)

I am highly motivated and disciplined, somewhat extra-verted, and have a great sense of responsibility. I also have the super amazing ability to study for 8 hours straight with little to no intermission. Obviously, parental support was necessary, financially and otherwise . . . I do know that I am much more fortunate than most . . . and that any trials or setbacks I may have pale in comparison to a lot of situations faced by others. I am so grateful for having a healthy mind and body and supportive family. To not maximize every opportunity for development is out of the question for me. I want to do great things—and for that, I must work a great deal. (Entered program at age 15.)

I think the friends that I made here and at home have contributed the most to my success. They were always there for me when I needed help on a concept. They were there for me when I needed advice. I also think that my faith in God has helped me through a lot of hard times. I don't think I would have achieved success without the constant support I receive from God and my friends. (Entered program at age 15.)

The biggest factor, I think, is that I like school. I love to learn and am generally very motivated and disciplined in my work. I suppose the relative absence of external disturbances that would interfere with my schoolwork has also contributed some to my success. (Entered college at age 14.)

Personal qualities—study skills (not habits), maturity, and a good balance of introversion/extroversion; external influences—a good network of friends and family, and supportive professors and advisors. (Entered program at age 14.)

In the beginning, it was definitely the help of my mother that brought me success. I would have done fine without her, but she kept me motivated. After the beginning, it was my own motivation and interest that kept me pushing hard. I am a calm person, which helped me focus during academically stressful periods. (Entered college at age 14.)

determination to do well; patience (everything takes time, often more than you seem to have); and good organization, which saves so much time in the end. (Entered program at age 16.)

I was always very independent. Being able to do things on my own without looking to the crowd for encouragement has made me strong. I'm good at time management, which is absolutely critical in college. I've also had a few out-of-this-world phenomenal mentors along the way ... [who] pushed me to expand my capabilities. I've also had some fantastic professors ... (Entered program at age 16.)

Both in my academics and sports career, I have achieved success through motivation and an almost unhealthy single-mindedness in my ability to focus. My parents were of great help in teaching me ... the value of hard work and the reading and over-the-top school projects that my father thrust on me, although incredibly aggravating at the time, have definitely been of use to me now that I am more or less an adult. (Entered program at age 16.)

Support from my parents was definitely critical. Mom proof-read nearly all of my papers (which I would e-mail her). I hate to have to mention it, but without my parents' and grand-parents' financial support, I also wouldn't have been able to attend the program. My parents also provided emotional support.... Understanding and sympathetic faculty members were also crucial to my ability to succeed. . . . I'm able to work intensely for short periods of time and that was the only way I could succeed academically. (Entered program at age 16.)

My seventh-grade math teacher once described me as a 35-year-old CEO trapped in an eighth grader's body, so my maturity has definitely contributed to my success since many of my other traits stem from it. I am independent, self-moti-vated, and organized. Above all, I manage my time well and I do not procrastinate ... (Entered program at age 16.)

I am highly motivated and disciplined, somewhat extra-verted, and have a great sense of responsibility. I also have the super amazing ability to study for 8 hours straight with little to no intermission. Obviously, parental support was necessary, financially and otherwise . . . I do know that I am much more fortunate than most . . . and that any trials or setbacks I may have pale in comparison to a lot of situations faced by others. I am so grateful for having a healthy mind and body and supportive family. To not maximize every opportunity for development is out of the question for me. I want to do great things—and for that, I must work a great deal. (Entered program at age 15.)

I think the friends that I made here and at home have contributed the most to my success. They were always there for me when I needed help on a concept. They were there for me when I needed advice. I also think that my faith in God has helped me through a lot of hard times. I don't think I would have achieved success without the constant support I receive from God and my friends. (Entered program at age 15.)

The biggest factor, I think, is that I like school. I love to learn and am generally very motivated and disciplined in my work. I suppose the relative absence of external disturbances that would interfere with my schoolwork has also contributed some to my success. (Entered college at age 14.)

Personal qualities—study skills (not habits), maturity, and a good balance of introversion/extroversion; external influences—a good network of friends and family, and supportive professors and advisors. (Entered program at age 14.)

In the beginning, it was definitely the help of my mother that brought me success. I would have done fine without her, but she kept me motivated. After the beginning, it was my own motivation and interest that kept me pushing hard. I am a calm person, which helped me focus during academically stressful periods. (Entered college at age 14.)

I was emotionally very immature, but aside from this, I had many advantages. I was focused, ambitious, enjoyed learning, and was intellectually very serious. I was comfortable with adults and spent a lot of time talking to my teachers who were very supportive. My parents were very supportive, as well, and so were a small number of close friends ... (Entered college at age 14.)

The support of my parents (especially financial) certainly made it possible. Personally, I think I had the innate ability and the motivation to put in a lot of hard work. Professors were very helpful, as well. (Entered program at age 13.)

Parent Perspectives About Factors That Promote Success

Parents also contributed their impressions of factors that promoted a successful adjustment to college.

Our daughter's emotional stability, high maturity level, excellent memory, hunger for knowledge, and the program support all helped.

His maturity and love for learning; his faith in God and strong moral beliefs; and love and support from parents, grandparents, aunts, uncles, cousins, teachers, and friends.

My daughter has always been self-motivated. She simply had to do her best in every academic challenge. I remember trying to get her to "lighten up" a bit, but it was to no avail. She was lucky to have the help and support of her TAG teachers who were instrumental in finding information about early entrance programs.

My child is self-motivated, mature for his age, and has the ability to focus very well. He can resist peer pressure and is self-confident. Also, being in Model United Nations in different leadership positions has helped him to become a confident, self-assured person. We are certain that support from parents/family, and having his sister as his role model have played an important part.

Our daughter had lived and gone to school in two very different cities—town and country—and each time had to separate from either a mom or dad, so she was used to leaving home. She likes responsibility and being her own boss. I never really had to shepherd her through school. She took care of herself.

I would like to claim support [was responsible for her success], but I must admit that my child's success is due all to her effort to learn and utilize the environment and resources that were made available to her.

Helpful personal characteristics were her strong focus on studies and being able to prioritize her time. As she puts it, "homework for me is not an option!" She also sets high goals for herself. She had strong support from her immediate family, friends, and relatives who lived close to campus. She also had support from the dorm directors and program administrators.

My son brought his own highly developed sense of purpose and a strong desire to learn to college with him. These qualities were essential to his success. I know many young people who go to college after high school simply because they are expected to and because they don't have anything better to do. Many hope that something in college will finally inspire them. My son never had this problem, even as a ninth grader. He knew then what he liked and he was already inspired to learn—what he lacked was the proper environment for him to do so.

I feel strongly that the two most important elements of his success were (1) . . . that neither his parents nor his formal educators stifled or hindered his extraordinary intellectual curiosity . . . and (2) we managed to keep him intellectually stimulated, supported his musical talent, and took him with us traveling. He was always very intense, focused, [and] intellectually but not socially perceptive. We played to his strengths.

Taking classes that are on her level and support from the program.

My daughter is intellectually very gifted and mature enough to be independent.

An innate drive to exceed educational expectations ... good health habits and personal grooming (not over the top, but sensible), parental support and expectations, and good support from the program.

Personal characteristics: conscientious, responsible, willingness to use feedback, sense of humor, empathic sensitivity, and looks for deeper meanings to things; environmental influences: daily phone contact with parents and best friend from CTY camp, four particularly inspiring and supportive professors, weekly psychotherapy, . . . and changing roommates.

Student Perspectives About Factors That Detract From Success

Students were asked to identify both internal and environmental factors that hindered them from achieving success. Although most of the students considered their college experiences successful, the vast majority of student respondents were able to identify factors that prevented them from having a smoother adjustment to college.

My biggest problem, by far, was laziness. I was not all used to working for success. In high school I had never studied or paid the slightest attention in class, but most of my grade was based on simple multiple-choice or fill-in-the-blank tests so I was able to use very good reasoning and memorization abilities to make up for an utter lack of actual work or knowledge. I didn't realize at the time that college uses different skills; just being smart isn't enough. You still have to put forth a sustained and concerted effort of pure work. At age 15, I was totally unaccustomed to any work harder than taking out the garbage, and assumed that I could just skate through on raw mental ability. Another serious factor in my failure was my decision to live on campus. I was so enthralled with the lack of any external authority telling me to do my homework and go to bed on time that I never considered that I might actually need to work and sleep. (Entered college at age 15.)

I have always been badly organized. My study habits only improved about 2–3 years ago. I had to learn the art of studying. It's not something you know innately. (Entered program at age 14.)

It is important to remember to study. Coming from a high school environment where I didn't have to study, it was very hard to get in the habit of studying. (Entered program at age 17.)

It was poor study habits that brought me down. . . . Also, my Calc II professor was pretty bad, but that's no excuse. (Entered program at age 17.)

Personal qualities: poor study habits and ego (sometimes I am too full of myself); external influences: a lack of certain opportunities at the university (e.g., connections to research, strong premed advising). (Entered program at age 14.)

I think my tendency to put things off has hurt me . . . (Entered program at age 15.)

Procrastination is definitely the biggest detracting factor in my experience. I'm naturally inclined to procrastinate anyway, but there are always people around to talk to and always the drama of your fellow students (I once had a housemate who broke up with her boyfriend 2–3 times a day with a few "real break ups" over the course of the year). . . . (Entered program at age 16.)

Poor time management skills primarily detracted from my success. I would often find myself with less time than I'd hoped for to read a book or write a paper. (Entered program at age 17.)

A lack of time. It's hard to work and go to school and have time to do the best I could. (Entered program at age 17.)

There were some difficult spots along the road, but I let my personal life get in the way. As well, I am a procrastinator, but I have learned my lessons. That is also why I am glad I came here first. It's a wonderful transition before I hit the big time universities. It's a time to learn what works and what doesn't. (Entered program at age 16.)

Other students and the dormitory environment. (Entered program at age 17.)

At times I put friends and social events before education. . . . The hall was loud and students were immature, but this was minor. Most of the students were grade-motivated instead of learning-motivated. (Entered program at age 16.)

Distractions: peers, my boyfriend, and extracurriculars; over-loading/breakdowns: mental breaks, whether caused by lack of sleep or too much stress definitely detracted from my success. (Entered program at age 16.)

During my first year in the program, I think I was somewhat distracted by a boy. I spent way too much time on AIM and on the phone with him and my schoolwork suffered a bit. I sometimes have bad study habits . . . (Entered program at age 13.)

The worst part about college is that it is fun—almost too much fun. Would you rather continue studying at 2 a.m. or go with your friends to drench someone with cold water? The choice is very easy. The bonds you develop and the strength of the camaraderie in dorms can often be a distraction. (Entered program at age 16.)

When I feel like I need to be better than others or filled with pride, that's when I get distracted from my definition of success. (Entered program at age 17.)

Being a perfectionist may have hurt me during various aspects of my college experience. (Entered program at age 15.)

I probably could have been more sociable while here. . . . If anything, I think I may have been too focused on my classes. This year, however, I have learned to relax. I now know that the world will not end if I stop by someone's room for an hour to chat on a weeknight. (Entered program at age 16.)

I had an aversion to formal events, and since I live far away from campus, I was not able to participate as fully in social events as I would have liked. Also, I love reading, perhaps a bit too much, to the point where it may have detracted from other things. (Entered program at age 13.)

As someone in an early college environment, I am forced to prove myself credible and on par with other college students who are older than me. The problem is, not only did we (early college students) skip 2 years of academic work, we're also working twice as hard (or believe that we are doing so). Social skills are often forgotten and are sacrificed, and I think it's a major failure in our college's goal. (Entered program at age 15.)

Parent Perspectives About Factors That Detract From Success

Parents were quite candid about what they perceived to be detrimental to their children's success in college. Here are some of their responses.

Distractions in the residence hall and, because of his age, lack of judgment to avoid getting into situations that he may not be ready to handle.

Our daughter ... did find dorm life to be distracting. Due to her late enrollment, she was roomed away from the rest of the female early entrants on a different floor.

Too many video games distracted her from concentrating on her studies. She got sidetracked.

The boyfriend my daughter had the first 2 years was a distraction.

My daughter held her own amidst peers who thought being sexually active and hungover or high [was acceptable].

Problems arose from procrastination and poor prioritization/time management. His first girlfriend was a distraction.

My daughter procrastinates. It makes every paper and every concert a crisis. I don't think waiting to go to college would improve this. I think she'll always tend to procrastinate. If anything, the program was a little more tolerant of this than most schools would be.

My child had a history of poor study habits and organizational skills, which were problems that were overcome [in college].

First year: The study habits were almost nonexistent. He still doesn't write down any assignments on a calendar. He is proud that he can do it all in his head and not forget! ... He admitted playing video games all night sometimes with dorm mates. The Sony Playstation did not go back with him the second year.

Even in college production was a struggle. Because he could take a lighter class load (three classes instead of four per quarter) he was able to succeed. [Because] our son was 13 when he entered college, it took him many years to establish sound study habits ...

She had to adjust her time organization. Given the fact that the quarter system goes much faster, she had to commit to a stricter schedule.

Poor study habits—when you have always "breezed" through school, it's hard to learn to have to study. But, try telling them that! Time management is a factor. For example, this quarter all of her classes are after 2 p.m., so the inclination is to sleep until noon, not to get up and work. Also, the attitude that some of the classes were "just" GE and/or required classes. The fact that she has no clear goal, so can't always see the "why" of a particular class. And, the social aspect—having too much fun to work hard.

Anxiety.

Difficulties that my son still confronts are basic to his character.

Mental health issues have been an ongoing concern.

Was Early Entrance to College Responsible for Failure?

When a traditional college student fails academically or has a negative college experience, it is disappointing. When this happens to an early entrant (even though it is rare), his or her parents' reaction may have the added dimensions of guilt and regret for permitting their child to take this unusual path. Although research has demonstrated that groups of early entrants do extremely well academically without concomitant social and emotional problems, we know that some individual early entrants do not adjust well to college (Brody, Muratori, & Stanley, 2004). In these rare cases, everyone wonders, "Was early entrance to college responsible for the student's failure?" This fear prevents some families from considering early entrance as a viable option when their children actually might be good candidates for it; but, let's face it, when things don't work out, it is natural to wonder if the student's adjustment and experiences would have been better if he or she had waited the extra year or two before entering college full time. Although we don't have a crystal ball to determine exactly how one's experience will unfold as an early entrant, we also cannot be 100% certain how staying longer in an unchallenging high school setting would impact this same student academically, socially, and emotionally. As I mentioned in the previous chapter, all one can do is weigh the options carefully and then make a decision based on information that is available.

With that said, in my experience, it is inaccurate to say that early college entrance can lead to failure. Rather, it is the "fit" between a student's educational and social/emotional needs and a specific curricular strategy and educational environment that influences how well or poorly that student adjusts. To illustrate this point, I will share a few examples of students who were not well-matched to their educational programs/settings.

One bright young woman enrolled in an early entrance program after she completed 11th grade; however, shortly after starting college, she discovered that she was extremely homesick, especially for her high school sweetheart who was still completing his high school education back home (several hours away). Despite her excellent GPA during her first year of college, her emotional issues felt so overpowering to her that she transferred to a college much closer to home. Upon making this change, she said:

> It's a huge stress reliever! I'm so much more happy and focused now that I can see my boyfriend on a regular basis. I find it's easier to get stuff done on the weekends now that I take time to go home and be with him. Despite the fact that it takes a large portion of the weekend, it makes the remaining time more productive than a weekend without him could be.

Even though the college to which she transferred had fewer course offerings than the university and was not regarded as prestigious, she felt the fit was much better in certain ways—in ways that were important to her. Aside from the appeal of its proximity to home, the campus was much smaller and the professors seemed more approachable, which was important to her. So, was early entrance a mistake in this case? Neither the student nor her mother regretted her year in the early entrance program; however, in retrospect, they believed that the ideal path for her would have been to enroll a year early at the college to which she eventually transferred. This example underscores the importance of selecting a suitable college, whether one enters early or enters at the traditional time. The topic of college selection will be explored in the next two chapters.

When young entrants fail academically in college, a natural assumption is that staying in high school would have been the wiser choice. Certainly there are instances in which that may be true, but there are other instances in which that may not be the case. Unfortunately, unproductive academic, social, and emotional patterns may be set into motion long before a student considers early entrance. Consider the case of one young entrant who started college after his junior year and failed academically to the extent that he was required to withdraw from the university for a certain period of time. Despite his struggles, he expressed no regrets,

> I may not have been successful academically, but nothing can replace everything I learned that first year. I think if I had stayed in high school, I probably would have become even more apathetic and would have been unsuccessful. I probably would have been unruly and in trouble a lot because I had nothing to do. I just can't think of any positives coming from my senior year.

Another young man who entered college one year early had a similar experience. Even though his attendance in classes and GPA plummeted due to a serious bout of depression, he believed that entering college early was a better option for him than remaining in high school. In his words:

> I can't imagine that I would have done anything remarkably different had I had one more year of

high school . . . other than really dislike high school that year, except for choir. I would have been in fluff courses, which I can't imagine would have prepared me for college courses.

The latter two examples suggest that gifted underachievers may have difficulties whether they remain in high school and graduate with their high school class, go to college early, or start college at the traditional time (after their senior year when they are a bit older). In fact, many of the factors that hinder the academic, social, and emotional adjustment of traditional college students are factors that have been cited in this chapter as detracting from the success of early entrants. For instance, researchers (e.g., Mathis & Lecci, 1999; Mooney, Sherman, & Lo Presto, 1991) have found academic locus of control to be positively correlated with total college adjustment. This certainly makes intuitive sense whether one is an early entrant or an older student. Those who take responsibility for their learning are in a much stronger position to make the most out of college. It follows that those who have an external locus of control and who don't take responsibility for their learning are at a disadvantage.

The two students mentioned above who failed academically did not take charge of their college experience. One attributed his refusal to participate in his education (he literally stopped attending classes) to the flawed educational system, which resulted in self-sabotage. The other student who had a reputation in high school as being a top student without having to study got off to a shaky start academically in college. He described the contrast between his high school and first-year college experiences:

> In high school, I can't ever remember a time when I was challenged. I probably studied at most an hour per week during high school. Obviously in college . . . no matter how smart an individual may be, he or she has to put in 2 to 3 hours per day [of studying] if not more. So, I came to college without any study skills whatsoever. I really didn't have any direction as far as time management

went. When I was in high school, I was free to spend my time however I wished because I knew I didn't have to study for tests or papers. . . . In college, oftentimes a midterm test will comprise of 3 or 4 months worth of lectures and notes and study groups.

Lacking the self-discipline and time management and study skills to get back on track academically, this student found his niche with other students who were more interested in partying than studying. Months earlier, this young man could not have predicted that his behavior would spiral out of control and would lead to academic failure. He clearly did not appear to have an internal locus of control. Other factors, such as his lack of clarity about goals, his reluctance to seek help and use available resources on campus, and motivational deficits, also contributed to the problems he encountered in college. Although one might conclude that his adjustment to college was not successful, he and his parents felt "certain the early entrance decision was the right one." As he stated, "at the time of the decision, it would have been ridiculous to make another choice."

Chance Factors

My observations from working with students, parents, and clients over the past several years, as well as my own experiences, have led me to believe that control is a fundamental need that people have. Some individuals develop problems resulting from their desire for an excessive amount of control, whereas others develop issues stemming from a lack of control and feelings of powerlessness. Whatever the case is—whether we have too much, too little, or just the perfect amount of it, we all hunger for a sense of control. It is no wonder, then, that anxiety increases (and skyrockets for some) when something unexpected happens. We will call these unexpected happenings *chance factors*.

There are times when chance factors (positive or negative) exert influence in the lives of early entrants. To cite a positive example, one student who was a phenomenal athlete entered college after her junior year of high school. After only one semester, she left the program because she was invited to reside at the Olympic Training Center to focus more intensively on her sport. She never anticipated that she would be afforded this wonderful opportunity. On the other end of the spectrum of unexpected factors, one young entrant was stalked for a few months by a disturbed classmate. Without question, being stalked is not an experience that one expects to have when leaving for college. Even though this student maintained her superb GPA, she was distracted and upset throughout this period. It understandably cast a dark cloud over her otherwise positive college experience. During his first year in college, another young entrant experienced the tragic loss of a high school friend who died in a car accident back home. This incident, in combination with his pervasive unhappiness resulting from his disappointment with certain professors in his major field of study, the size of the campus, and his incompatible roommate, exacerbated his sense of homesickness. He eventually transferred to a different college where his "social life more than bloomed, it exploded" after he joined a fraternity. He maintained excellent grades and in virtually all respects had a successful and rewarding college experience.

Running To or Running From?

Making a successful adjustment to college depends on a multitude of internal and external/environmental factors, some of which have already been explored and others that will be presented later in the book. Pinpointing the personal qualities and other factors that will likely impact success is of paramount importance. One final question to reflect on is whether one is running toward an opportunity that seems exciting or if one is running or escaping from an unpleasant experience in high school.

Comments From the Experts

Gifted-child experts were asked to respond to the following question: We often make a distinction between early entrants who are running to an exciting and challenging opportunity and those who are running from or escaping something negative in middle or high school. What advice can you offer prospective early entrants who fall into the second category? Their responses are found below.

Rather than running away from a high school environment where they lack friends or any interest in schoolwork, successful early college students usually enter college for positive reasons. They look forward to the challenge of more rigorous content than their high school offers and the flexibility to pursue their interests in greater depth. Socially, they welcome interacting with more mature college students who share their intellectual interests. In contrast, those who are running away from what they don't like about high school are likely to take their problems with them. Students who are having a great deal of trouble interacting with peers should get counseling to help develop their social skills. If grades are poor, it may be boredom, but they need to be sure their study skills are solid before tackling the rigor of college courses. If they are dealing with depression, they should seek medical help and not assume a change in scene will cure it. Adjusting to college is challenging enough, especially for young college students, without taking these kinds of problems with them.

—Dr. Linda Brody, Director of the Julian C. Stanley Study of
Exceptional Talent (SET), Center for Talented Youth, Johns Hopkins
University, Baltimore, MD

This is a sensitive and serious issue. Is the student running away from something in [his or her] school or [his or her] age-peer group (something environmental) or [is he or she] running away from something in [him- or herself] (something intrapersonal)?

If you are escaping from a curriculum treadmill where you spend your time trudging over ground you have covered countless times before, acceleration of any kind can give you an escape route to a more rewarding terrain. If you are escaping from classmates who don't understand you and who may envy, resent, or ever fear what they don't understand, then being with students who are closer to your own levels of intellectual and emotional maturity may give you access to a whole new world of relationships.

However, if you are consciously or unconsciously running away from something you don't understand about yourself or something you find hard to accept in yourself, then this can be problematic. Sometimes counselors can be of great assistance in helping us understand the "direction" in which we are running and our reasons for doing so.

—*Professor Miraca U. M. Gross, Director, Gifted Education Research, Resource and Information Centre (GERRIC), The University of New South Wales, Sydney, Australia*

While exiting a negative situation may need to be done quickly, it should still be done as purposefully as possible. Examining the reasons why a student wants to move on is very important to avoid history repeating itself in the next educational setting. It's important for students and parents to work together to explore options. Early college entrance may be appealing in many ways, but it's important to understand the relative strengths and weaknesses of the choice to attend college early. There are many variations of entering college early, ranging from taking a class or two, to enrolling full time and living on campus. Early college programs may also be an option, as they are designed for students entering college at least a year or two early.

—*Ms. Colleen Harsin, Director of Programs, Davidson Institute for Talent Development, Reno, NV*

If you are running away from a bad situation toward early college entrance, you have to ask yourself if you are willing to put up with the downsides of your new situation. For example, are you prepared to do the work involved in an accelerated learning environment? Have you considered the potential negatives of the new social situation? Early entrance candidates who want to escape a difficult situation really need to contemplate the possible challenges of the new situation, because there will inevitably be some. If after reflection, the new situation is still preferable, then go for it.

—*Dr. Paula Olszewski-Kubilius, Director, Center for Talent Development, Northwestern University, Evanston, IL*

It's important to examine the reasons why a student might want to escape a poorly fitting middle or high school situation. If it is because the student truly is more advanced than fellow students and consequently having a hard time finding compatible friends, then early entry to college can be considered. If the school is truly just basically boring or the student is on the outs with [his or her] social group for other reasons, then a change of schools, a modest degree of acceleration (e.g., skipping eighth grade or taking online courses in an area of high interest) or finding an area of talent or even a hobby to develop (more) seriously are better options and also may afford a pool of potential friends who are more likely to share the student's interest and to "talk the same language." Students who go to summer programs offered by the talent search organizations often get "revved up," as well. Sometimes, students who are running from an unhappy school situation are unhappy for other reasons—poor social skills, family dynamics, mental health issues—that deserve attention on their own and don't necessarily imply a school change.

—*Dr. Nancy Robinson, Professor Emerita of Psychiatry and Behavioral Sciences, and cofounder of The Halbert and Nancy Robinson Center for Young Scholars, University of Washington, Seattle, WA*

Conclusion

Success is a multifaceted concept that cannot be defined easily or measured using only one standard. Due to many factors including one's abilities, interests, priorities, cultural and personal values, personality, expectations, family history, politics, and stakeholder role (e.g., student, parent, early entrance program administrator, high school teacher, principal, or guidance counselor), one individual's definition of success invariably will differ from another individual's definition. And, who wants the job of deciding whose definition is correct and whose is incorrect? I certainly don't! In my opinion, success, like beauty, is in the eye of the beholder.

As prospective early entrants define success for themselves, they must begin to think about the conditions under which they are able to achieve success and perform optimally. Those who need or who are accustomed to a lot of support may benefit from entering a special program that is tailored to the unique needs of early entrants. These programs will be described in Chapter 6.

Early Entrance Programs in the United States

Focus Questions for Students:

- How do you think you would react to being in a program with other early entrants? Would you enjoy the camaraderie?

- Would you feel constrained by receiving more support than other freshmen on campus or would you be comforted to receive the extra support and guidance that a special program provides?

- Have you had your heart set on attending a particular college/university? If you enter a program that expects you to earn your 4-year degree at the university in which the program is housed, how do you suppose you would feel to give up on the idea of attending your "dream school" for your undergraduate education?

- What aspects of each program appeal to you the most and least?

Focus Questions for Parents:

- How do you think your child would react to being in a program with other talented young entrants?

- How do you think your son or daughter would feel about receiving support from an early entrance program, which students outside of the program would not receive?

Focus Questions for Parents, continued:

• How would you feel sending your child to a special program that offers extra support and guidance as opposed to a regular college/university?

• What aspects of each program appeal to you most and least as a parent?

The first few chapters of this book are intended to help you answer the question, "Should I (or my child) enter college early on a full-time basis?" Chapters 6 and 7 are devoted to exploring how to find the right fit in a college assuming the option of early college entrance is still on the table. The task of narrowing down options and finding a college or university that fulfills your (or your child's) specific needs may feel overwhelming at first. So, where should you begin?

Important Tasks for Prospective Early Entrants

A logical first step is to figure out precisely what your specific needs are and to prioritize them if possible. After all, how can you find a learning environment that is well-matched to your needs unless you have a pretty clear idea of what your needs are and what you are looking for in a college? If you are not sure about what you need in order to be successful in college, don't panic. You are in good company with many other academically talented students who have not yet clarified their needs. Nevertheless, because you are facing a major decision that will likely impact the next few years of your life, now would be a good time to start thinking about what you need in order to thrive academically and personally. College may seem like an abstract concept in some ways right now (especially if you have never taken a course on a college campus before), however, the quality of your college experience will be affected by concrete decisions you

make. Some of these decisions must be made before you start college, whereas others will be made after you are a fully matriculated student. These decisions will be addressed in subsequent chapters.

As you gain clarity about your unique needs, the next critical task is for you to consider whether you want to enter college early through a special program that is designed specifically for early entrants or if you want to enter college on your own without the support of a special program. Whereas a discussion of the latter can be found in Chapter 7, the remainder of this chapter will focus on selected early entrance programs in the United States.

What Is an Early Entrance Program and Why Join One?

Special programs have been established in various colleges and universities around the nation to accommodate the unique academic, social, and emotional needs of academically talented students who are ready for college early. These programs vary on a number of dimensions, yet share some important features, perhaps the most apparent one being that the program administrators and staff tend to have a deeper understanding than most educators of the issues related to and implications of being a younger-than-typical student in college. Another common feature of these programs is that they attract bright students who share the desire to get a jumpstart on their college educations.

From a socialization standpoint, these programs provide their participants with opportunities to meet other early entrants like themselves, which may be a welcome change for those who have felt isolated or socially out of place in high school. That is not to imply that most young entrants leave high school early or, in rare instances, miss high school altogether because they do not fit in socially. Many have strong social skills and claim to get along very well with their high school classmates. They simply feel starved educationally and need to move on to a much more challenging learning environment. Another caveat is that one cannot assume all early entrants will develop friendships with each other simply because they share the experience of being early entrants. Personality and value clashes, for instance, can preclude two students from socializing with or liking each other. However, this common denominator of experiencing early college entrance can help program participants to break the ice and establish some peer relationships in their initial months on campus, which may be comforting and reassuring to them during this critical time period in their adjustment to college. I must add that in some cases, friendships that blossom in these programs are enduring and very meaningful.

In addition to peer support, counseling and guidance provided by staff and special program activities tend to be key perks of joining an early entrance program. To reiterate, the purpose of these programs is to assist in the academic, social, and emotional development of their participants; however, the programs vary in the amount and type of support they offer, which to an extent may depend on how radically accelerated their students tend to be. Clearly, a student who leaves high school after completing 11th-grade coursework has different needs than a brilliant 13-year-old who has been homeschooled because his or her needs were never met at school. If both of these students decided to enter college early through a special program, they would find their optimal fit in different programs that were tailored to their respective academic, social, and emotional needs.

A prime example of a program that is specifically designed for students who require radical acceleration is the University of Washington's Early Entrance Program (EEP), which is offered through the Halbert and Nancy Robinson Center for Young Scholars. Aware that the social and emotional maturity of these young students may lag behind their intellectual and academic development, the program staff is highly trained to deal with the unique needs of radically accelerated students.

The EEP, which at present accepts 16 extremely able students per year who must be younger than 15, is

> a two-step program consisting of one year of Transition School, an intensive college preparatory program taught at the Robinson Center, and subsequent full-time enrollment at the University of Washington, typically beginning with one or more courses during the Transition School year. (The Halbert and Nancy Robinson Center for Young Scholars, 2005, ¶ 8)

Given the young age of the students, the program is not designed to be residential. When the students are ready to move into a residence hall (usually 2 or more years after they join the EEP), they are allowed to make that transition; however, until that time, they remain commuters. Clearly, this has implications for the parents of these young entrants who often must chauffeur them to and from the university and who may even go as far as to relocate to the Seattle area if they do not already live within driving distance of the university.

To serve the needs of students who are not candidates for radical acceleration, the Robinson Center established another early entrance program in which academically talented students enroll in college after they have completed the 10th grade. At present, the Academy for Young Scholars offers 35 students per year admission to the University of Washington and the UW Honors Program 2 years ahead of their high school peers. A special feature of the academy is the Bridge Program, which includes three components: "an orientation at Camp Indionola, the Jump-Start lecture course and discussion sections during September, and the Fall Quarter Seminar/Writing Link" (The Halbert and Nancy Robinson Center, 2005, ¶ 6). Contact information for these two programs can be found in the appendix.

Dr. Nancy Robinson, Professor Emerita of Psychiatry and Behavioral Sciences, and cofounder of The Halbert and Nancy Robinson Center for Young Scholars at the University of Washington, designed the EEP and has had a distinguished

99

career researching the needs of radical accelerants. She was asked the following question:

In your many years of interacting with early entrants and observing their academic, social, and emotional adjustment to college, did you notice any similarities and patterns among students who did not fare well in the EEP and at UW? If so, what were they?

NR: We try (tried) to be very careful to admit only students who are not only bright enough to handle the academic demands (I don't think we ever made a mistake there), but mature in their outlook, pretty well-organized in their lives, and self-motivated to succeed. Still, some issues that are hard to preassess did get in the way of a few students' lack of success.

The most common was the existence of an agenda at home that we had not been told about. Typically, this consisted of strife between the parents that simply sapped all the spare psychic energy a student had. Occasionally, this was a hidden conflict between the parents about whether the student should come into the program, with one parent undermining efforts, but more often it was a more general issue between the parents that might result in their divorcing. For a few low-income families, the home issues had to do with chores or care of younger siblings that the student was expected to continue (often combined with a rather long commute because there is so little low-income housing in the Seattle community), so that there just wasn't time or support to devote to the 4 to 5 hours of homework our students were expected to do. It was not just the time demands, though—for some of our most successful students continued in a time-demanding talent area such as music or dance—it had more to do with a combination of support, organization, and expectations for the role the student was expected to play at home.

Another very occasional surprise was the emergence of a subtle learning disability such as ADD or working memory span for which the student had been able to compensate in a less demanding situation. When we were able to catch this right away and parents followed through, sometimes we were able to make it work, but often parents were disbelieving because the student had [previously] done so well, and so they didn't pursue prompt diagnosis and intervention.

And, also very occasionally, a student just didn't believe us when we warned [him or her] of the rigor of the program, because everything else [he or she] had been told would be "hard" had proved to be easy—and [he or she] just didn't choose to work as hard as [he or she] needed to.

The development of these two programs through the Robinson Center reinforces the point that all early entrance programs cannot and should not look the same or be structured in the same manner. To illustrate the similarities and differences between programs, brief descriptions of several other prominent early entrance programs will be provided in the next section with the added bonus of advice from the directors and administrators of the programs.

An Overview of Selected Early Entrance Programs

As seen in *A Nation Deceived*, Tables 1 and 2 (Brody et al., 2004) provide a listing of selected residential and commuter early entrance programs in the nation and provide basic information about the programs' special characteristics. Although this is not an exhaustive list of the programs, it should give you a flavor of the variation that exists among them. More detailed descriptions of nine early entrance programs are found below.

The Advanced Academy of Georgia (AAG)

Located in Carrollton, GA, on the campus of the University of West Georgia (UWG), AAG is a residential

Table 1

Selected *Residential* Early Entrance Programs in the U.S.				
Program	**Inception Date**	**Grade at Entry**	**Issues H.S. Diploma?**	**Special Characteristics**
State University of West Georgia **Advanced Academy of Georgia**	1995	11th or 12th	No*	• All university programs are available to AAG students, who are automatically in Honors College. • AAG offers many leadership, social, and residence hall activities/opportunities. • AAG students reside in honors residence hall and are supervised by live-in staff.
University of North Texas **Texas Academy of Mathematics and Science**	1988	11th	Yes	• Strong emphasis is on math and science. • TAMS has a mostly required curriculum. • TAMS has approximately 25 clubs and service organizations. • TAMSters have their own large residence hall and are supervised by live-in staff. • TAMS only admits residents of Texas.
Middle Georgia College **Georgia Academy of Mathematics, Engineering, & Science**	1997	11th or 12th	No*	• Focus is on preparing GAMES students in technical fields. • GAMES offers students many enrichment activities (e.g., 10 field trips every semester). • GAMES students have their own residence hall and are supervised by live-in staff. • MGC is a 2-year college, so all GAMES graduates transfer to 4-year institutions.
Lamar University **Texas Academy of Leadership in the Humanities**	1994	Typically, 11th	Yes	• Emphasis is on the humanities and on the development of character and leadership skills. • TALH students have a community service requirement. • TALH arranges for students to attend plays, concerts, leadership programs, and cultural events, and offers students traditional high school activities. • TALH students reside in their own new privately operated, apartment-style, gated dormitory with live-in staff. • TALH admits only residents of Texas.
Northwest Missouri State University **Missouri Academy of Science, Mathematics, and Computing**	2000	11th	Yes	• Focus is on technical subjects. • MASMC students are required to study 2 hours/night Sunday–Thursday. • MASMC students are permitted to organize clubs under the guidance of a staff/faculty advisor. • Community service is encouraged. • MASMC students reside in a residence hall and have full-time staff to assist them.
Clarkson University **Clarkson School Bridging Year Program**	1978	12th	No**	• Focus is on meeting high school requirements and researching future college options. • CS sponsors "family dinners" for students and staff. • Field trips and special events are scheduled. • CS students live in suites in their own residence hall and are supervised by live-in staff.

Note. Adapted from "Early Entrance to College: Academic, Social, and Emotional Considerations," by L. E. Brody, M. C. Muratori, and J. C. Stanley, in *A Nation Deceived: How Schools Hold Back America's Brightest Students* (pp. 98–100), by N. Colangelo, S. G. Assouline, and M. U. M. Gross (Eds.), 2004, Iowa City, IA: The Connie Belin & Jacqueline N. Blank International Center for Gifted Education and Talent Development. Copyright ©2004 by The Connie Belin & Jacqueline N. Blank International Center for Gifted Education and Talent Development. Adapted with permission.

Selected *Residential* Early Entrance Programs in the U.S.

Program	Inception Date	Grade at Entry	Issues H.S. Diploma?	Special Characteristics
Mary Baldwin College **Program for the Exceptionally Gifted**	1985	8th–11th	No	• PEG students are urged to take core college requirements during the first 2 years before pursuing specific majors/degree programs. • Students are not automatically in Honors Program. • PEG students have several leadership opportunities (e.g., committees, peer advising). • Staggered approach is used: PEG students gain more freedom over time. They reside on campus for 4 years. Younger PEG students receive more intensive supervision and support.
Bard College **Simon's Rock College**	1966	Typically 11th or 12th	No*	• SRC is a fully accredited liberal arts college that offers associates or bachelors degrees in a variety of disciplines. • SRC has been affiliated with Bard College since 1979 (BC provides students with additional academic resources).*** • SRC promotes a holistic, interdisciplinary approach and offers small class sizes. • SRC sponsors cultural events and lecture/film series. • Students participate in community service and the Recreational Activities Program. • First-year students reside on campus.
University of Southern California **Resident Honors Program**	1961 (1984)****	12th	No*	• RHP students are encouraged to earn their undergraduate degrees from USC. • RHP students are automatically enrolled in the Honors Program and can take the Thematic Option honors core. • RHP students are incorporated into the larger USC community and are encouraged to participate in university-sponsored activities. • Some activities are sponsored by RHP. • RHP students reside with other honors students. Faculty-in-residence live in the residential learning community.
The University of Iowa **National Academy of Arts, Sciences, and Engineering**	1999	12th	No*	• NAASE students are encouraged to earn their undergraduate degrees from UI. • NAASE students take courses with other UI students from the time they enter the program. • NAASE students are automatically enrolled in the UI Honors Program. • NAASE students attend weekly study sessions. • NAASE students are encouraged to participate in UI clubs and activities as well as activities sponsored by NAASE and the Belin-Blank Center. • NAASE students reside in the honors residence hall and are supervised by live-in staff.

* Arrangements are made for the high school diploma to be granted by the student's high school.
** Students can earn a diploma from the state of New York.
*** But SRC is not near Bard College.
****Although RHP was established in 1961, a new administration implemented a scholarship program in 1984, and admissions standards were dramatically increased.

103

Table 2

Selected *Commuter* Early Entrance Programs in the U.S.				
Program	**Inception Date**	**Grade at Entry**	**Issues H.S. Diploma?**	**Special Characteristics**
University of Washington **Early Entrance Program**	1977	Typically, 8th	No	• 2-step program: 1 year Transition School (TS) followed by early entrance into UW. • TS/EEP students have access to special support services (e.g., academic advising), activities (e.g., drama society), and resources (student lounge). • TS students must be no more than 14 years old; students are usually between 12–14 years old at entry.
University of Washington **UW Academy for Young Scholars**	2001	11th	No	• Students attend Jump Start, a two-week program that helps to prepare them for the demands of college. • UW Academy students take special classes during their 1st quarter and receive special support services. • Students are encouraged to form a close social network within the academy and become active in the UW Honors Program.
California State University Los Angeles **Early Entrance Program**	1983	Typically, 9th	No*	• All qualified EEP applicants complete provisional summer courses. • Students have access to EEP resources: student lounge, computer lab, library, counseling services, etc. • 4th- and 5th-year students are "elders" who informally mentor younger students. • EEP students are encouraged to complete undergraduate degrees at CSULA. • EEP students can enter the program between the ages of 11–16.
Boston University **Boston University Academy**	1993	Typically, 8th or 9th	Yes	• BUA students take high school courses through 11th grade. • BUA students attend college-level courses on a part-time basis in 11th grade and on a full-time basis in 12th grade. • BUA offers a wide range of extracurricular activities (sports, performing arts, Model UN, Debate Club, Robotics Team, etc.).
Guilford College **Early College at Guilford**	2002	9th	Yes	• ECG students complete high school and the first 2 years of college in 4 years. • School offers 25 extracurricular clubs/organizations plus enrichment activities. • ECG is open only to students from the Guilford County School System.
Bard College **Bard High School Early College**	2001	9th	No**	• BHSEC students complete high school and the first 2 years of college in 4 years. • BHSEC is located 50 miles from the Bard College campus. • School offers many extracurricular clubs and opportunities. • BHSEC is open only to students from the New York City public school system.

Selected *Commuter* Early Entrance Programs in the U.S.				
Program	**Inception Date**	**Grade at Entry**	**Issues H.S. Diploma?**	**Special Characteristics**
Alaska Pacific University **Early Honors Program**	2000	12th	No***	• EHP uses "Block and Session" format: intensive focus on few subjects. • Program does not offer extracurricular activities (students can participate in high school or university clubs), • Study Abroad experience is emphasized. • EHP students complete a year of transferable college credit (1-year program).

* Arrangements can be made for students to take a high school proficiency examination.
** Students earn a Regents Diploma from the State of New York. In some early entrance programs that offer both high school and college courses, students are considered high school students through their senior year.
*** Arrangements are made for the high school diploma to be granted by the student's high school.

Note. Adapted from "Early Entrance to College: Academic, Social, and Emotional Considerations," by L. E. Brody, M. C. Muratori, and J. C. Stanley, in *A Nation Deceived: How Schools Hold Back America's Brightest Students* (p. 101), by N. Colangelo, S. G. Assouline, and M. U. M. Gross (Eds.), 2004, Iowa City, IA: The Connie Belin & Jacqueline N. Blank International Center for Gifted Education and Talent Development. Copyright ©2004 by The Connie Belin & Jacqueline N. Blank International Center for Gifted Education and Talent Development. Adapted with permission.

early entrance program for academically talented high school students from the United States. International students are also welcome to apply. As a rule, participants of AAG are admitted after their sophomore or junior year, although under special circumstances, younger students with exceptional abilities may be accepted into the program. Eligible to apply for both merit- and need-based scholarships, AAG students have the opportunity to earn remaining high school credits and accrue college credits at the same time by taking courses at the university. The university is a 4-year institution that offers more than 50 degree programs and that affords AAG students the opportunity to participate in the UWG's 2-2 Regent's Engineering Transfer Program with the Georgia Institute of Technology. Automatically qualified to enroll in the Honors College, AAG participants can assume leadership positions on the Honors Council and can avail themselves of small seminar classes, faculty mentoring, and research opportunities. As stated on AAG's Web site,

A hallmark of both West Georgia and the Advanced Academy is our emphasis on undergraduate research. Five of the last seven years West Georgia had more student research proposals accepted for presentation to the annual National Collegiate Honors Council

Conference (a highly competitive process) than any other institution in the country! Many of the West Georgia students attending and presenting at this conference were Academy students. (Advanced Academy of Georgia, 2002, ¶ 6)

AAG students reside together in Gunn Hall, which is reserved for students in the Academy and Honors College. Recently renovated, it reportedly has nicer amenities than other dormitories on campus and has a more personal and warm ambience (partly due to its smaller size). AAG students also have access to a number of special services including counseling and advising.

Admissions Criteria

The recommended standardized test scores for admission to the academy are 1150 minimum on the SAT (580 verbal; 530 math) or a minimum composite score of 25 on the ACT (25 English; 22 math). For more information about the application process and admission criteria, visit http://www.advancedacademy.org.

Comments by Ms. Susan Colgate, Director of AAG

1. What makes your program unique?

The Advanced Academy is unique in that outside of the residence hall in which they live, our students are fully integrated into the larger university community. With the exception of intercollegiate athletics and Greek social fraternities and sororities, AAG students are fully involved in all facets of campus life. Our students join the marching band, act in the West Georgia Theater Company productions, write for the student newspaper, perform in various musical ensembles, play chess with the chess club, compete on the College Bowl team, serve on campus committees, and join campus organizations. Our students have been president of the physics club, editor of the annual literary magazine, president of Residence

Life's Presidents' Council, and organizer and president of the campus future medical doctors' association.

We are also unique in that we are a component of the Honors College, and our students are Honors students, eligible for all the benefits of the Honors College: Honors classes that are small in size and taught across the curriculum, mentoring relationships with professors, early registration, and unprecedented opportunities for undergraduate research. Our students are encouraged to become involved with either an ongoing research project with a faculty member or one of their own design, again under faculty supervision. For 7 of the past 8 years, the University of West Georgia has had more student proposals accepted for presentation at the National Collegiate Honors Council Conference than any other institution in the country. Academy students' proposals are among those that have been submitted and accepted. Our students have attended other professional conferences around the country where they have presented their research findings.

Unlike many early entrance programs, we do not have our own faculty, and we do not have an established curriculum. Our students take regularly scheduled university classes and are advised according to their needs, interests, and levels of preparation and ability. Each student is advised and registered for classes individually, which allows for a great deal of personal attention and attending to individual differences. For example, our students' first semester university math classes range from College Algebra to Calculus II (or higher), depending on their past class work, achievements, and future plans. Also, many students qualify to skip freshman English and enroll in a sophomore-level Honors English Literature class (World, American, or British). If they earn an A or a B in this class, they receive credit for the freshman English 1101 and 1102 classes.

Also, somewhat unique is our diverse student body. The majority of students are from Georgia, but we accept students from out of state and from other countries. Our student body is not limited to those studying math or science; we have art, film, English, philosophy, pre-law, and psychology

107

majors living and studying with pre-med, biomedical engineering, nuclear engineering, physics, and math majors. It makes for a great mix, and our students are generous in their acceptance and support of one another.

Our residential hall program is unique in that we are very responsive to students' interests; much of our programming is student-driven. For example, we have our own residence hall newsletter, completely run by students. This year, the newsletter staff had the idea to sponsor a coffee house, during which students presented original short stories, poems, and artwork. Non-Academy students and several English professors were also invited to attend and participate. The event was very successful and won a programming award on campus.

We are also unique in that we occasionally accept highly able younger students after first carefully determining that they have the maturity and skills necessary to succeed in a residential, accelerative program.

2. For whom is AAG ideal? For whom is it not?

AAG is ideal for the mature, self-directed individual who wants to accelerate academically and experience something other than what they have in high school. I like to think of it as someone who wants to go toward something, not escape from something, whatever that may be. This individual would have existing time management and study skills, be motivated toward full participation in the program, have good self-discipline, love to learn, be adaptable, have good communication skills, and possess a high degree of self-knowledge.

AAG is not ideal for the individual who is not sufficiently mature; has emotional and/or behavioral problems; whose goal is to get away from something or otherwise has questionable motivation for applying; who has poor social skills; who is not disciplined; who is addicted to video games; and who is not able to make good decisions regarding bedtimes, eating, and other choices that are inherent in a residential program.

3. Obviously, you select students for the AAG with the expectation that they will succeed. What is your definition of success?

When this question is taken in its fullness, it is a diffi-cult question to answer as I think there are almost as many answers to this question as there are students. Looked at nar-rowly, there is the more standard definition of success that we expect from an early entrance program and its students—a "poster-girl or -boy" individual whose success is obvious and falls into expected areas: a scintillating intellect, academic excellence consistently manifesting at the top percentages, a stunning list of extracurriculars, and acceptance into a pres-tigious graduate or professional school. That student clearly demonstrates our reason for being and can be a joy to work with and to know. But, I would propose that there are other, equally important, if not so obvious, definitions of success. Students who discover true, visceral learning, who have to really think for the first time, who may struggle and not get by solely on their wits or innate abilities—even if they earn less than perfect 4.0 GPAs—exemplify a version of success. A student who enters with social skills or attitudes that cause us to occasionally apologize for him or her and offer counsel in more appropriate ways to act, but who leave us with the countenance, demeanor, and behaviors of a self-confident, happy, and pleasant-to-be-around individual is a success. An introverted, go-it-alone student who makes true friends, per-haps for the first time, is a success. And, so on. One problem with identifying too much with one definition of success is the disaffection and marginalization of students who do not fit that definition. I have noticed that students sometimes resent that their unique contributions are bypassed in favor of those that fit a predetermined mold.

4. What personal characteristics/qualities seem to help students succeed as early entrants?

Maturity, ability to withstand negative peer pressure, posi-tive outlook, independence, supportive and involved parents, either existing study and time management skills or the ability

109

to quickly learn them, either lots of energy or the ability to effectively use the energy they have, focus, personal goals and direction, dedication, clarity as to why they are in the program, self-discipline, confidence, feeling comfortable around and speaking with adults, and good moral judgment. The last item in the list does not emanate from any value judgments I may or may not make and does allow for individual determination, but comes from an observation that this attribute keeps kids out of trouble and focused.

5. What personal factors or characteristic/qualities hinder early entrants from succeeding in college?

The opposite or lack of items listed in Question 4.

6. What external/environmental factors seem to promote success among the AAG students?

Mentoring by professors, caring and accessible staff, the positive peer pressure that exists in the residence halls and encourages students to do and be their best, good relationships with parents (or finding other adults with whom to have meaningful relationships), campus resources (e.g., career counseling), and the exceptional sense of community we work hard to create and maintain and our students find in our residence hall.

7. What external/environmental factors hinder success among the AAG students?

Too much pressure from parents, pressure to fulfill parental expectations instead of being allowed to find their own way and passion, negativity, negative peer pressure, family problems, drama in the residence hall.

Clarkson School (CS)

A division of Clarkson University in Potsdam, NY, the Clarkson School offers a bridging year program for 50–80 students (from the United States and abroad) per year who have completed their junior-level coursework in high school and are ready for college one year early. The academic philosophy of the Clarkson School is:

> that it is essential to offer a curriculum that emphasizes increased proficiency with relevant technological skills, effective communication of ideas in both the written and spoken word, and the building and refining of analytical reasoning powers. Clarkson School students are encouraged to sample a wide variety of courses as they investigate prospective majors and explore career possibilities throughout their year. (Clarkson University, 2005b, ¶ 1)

In contrast to certain early entrance programs that intend for their students to earn bachelor's degrees from the host university, the Clarkson School makes no such assumption. Although some students may opt to continue their undergraduate studies at Clarkson University upon the completion of their bridging year experience, most go on to pursue degrees from other universities. Depending on the policies of their high schools, students may be able to receive a diploma directly from their high school or receive a General Equivalency Diploma from the state of New York. One caveat is that those seeking high school credit for their college coursework are not eligible for federal grants and loans; however, these students may apply for merit- and need-based scholarships through the Clarkson School.

Like all other Clarkson University students, early entrants attending this program have full access to university resources such as research laboratories and other facilities. They are permitted to participate in all intramural and certain intercollegiate sports and can avail themselves of faculty mentoring and advanced research opportunities. Program

111

staff help to facilitate a smooth transition by guiding the students through the college application process and offering them personalized attention and support.

Clarkson School students reside together:

> in wings of an undergraduate residence, in suites consisting of two rooms and one bath, shared by four students. Each of the floors has a common area furnished with couches, chairs, and used for socializing, studying, and meetings. A house advisor lives on each floor. Family dinners for staff, students, and house advisors provide an opportunity for everyone to get together regularly. (Clarkson University, 2005a, ¶ 11)

In addition to the family dinners, the program staff organizes special activities in the residence hall, as well as those outside of the residence hall (e.g., field trips).

Admissions Criteria

Acceptable standardized tests include the SAT or ACT. SAT-II test scores are optional. Although minimum tests scores are not indicated, the average SAT-I scores for the 2002–2004 classes were 597 Verbal and 620 Math. Those who intend to major in business or liberal arts should take four units of English, three units of math, and one unit of science prior to attending Clarkson. Students who want to major in engineering, science, and interdisciplinary engineering and management should complete four units of English, four units of math, and three to four units of science, including chemistry and physics. See http://www.clarkson.edu/tcs for more details.

Comments of Mr. Shailindar Singh, Interim Head of the Clarkson School, Director of Academic Counseling

1. What makes your early entrance program unique?

The Clarkson School is open to students from all over the country and all over the world. Ours is a program that brings students to college one year early and we encourage students to make applications to other colleges and universities while they study with us. There is no assumption or requirement that students will remain at Clarkson University following their Clarkson School experiences. We also have a longer history than most early entrance programs.

2. For whom is the Clarkson School ideal? For whom is it not?

The Clarkson School is ideal for the motivated learner who can't wait to get started on collegiate study. We're often a good choice for students who may be a bit bored in high school and/or will not be challenged by their senior years.

The Clarkson School is not ideal for students whose primary motivation for leaving high school early is something other than academics.

3. Obviously, you select students for the Clarkson School with the expectation that they will succeed. What is your definition of success?

This is a broad question, and it varies from student to student. Success depends on students' own goals and capacities. But, Clarkson School students typically outperform their freshmen peers.

4. Based on your observations and experience, what personal characteristics/qualities (e.g., ability to focus) seem to help students succeed as early entrants?

The students who perform at the highest academic levels manage their time well, demonstrate self-discipline, are resilient, and are continuously motivated. Nearly all college students, Clarkson School students included, face an adjustment period. Clarkson School students (by and large) make very successful adjustments and therefore outperform their peers.

113

5. In your view, what personal factors or characteristics/qualities (e.g., poor study habits) hinder early entrants from succeeding in college?

Students who do not learn to manage their time well; who initially lack self-discipline; and whose motivation is sporadic have taken longer to find success. Not every student comes to college with these favorable characteristics. Adjusting means developing them and most do so early on. Our program provides the academic support to nurture students during this adjustment period, if necessary. These can include counseling, advising, mentoring, and tutoring.

6. What external/environmental factors (e.g., supportive family) seem to promote success among the Clarkson School students?

Success among Clarkson School students is largely a question of opportunity and hard work. But, we also establish a sense of community here with family dinners, field trips, faculty mentoring, and plenty of interaction between students and supportive staff.

7. What external/environmental factors (e.g., distractions in residence hall) hinder success among the Clarkson School students?

I do not perceive environmental factors as hindering success here.

Early Entrance Program (EEP)

Similar to the University of Washington's Early Entrance Program (EEP), which is designed for radical accelerants, the Early Entrance Program (EEP) at California State University Los Angeles (CSULA) is a commuter program for students who would benefit from radical acceleration into college.

The following guidelines must be adhered to with regard to age at time of college entry:

> The Program allows qualified students as young as 11 years of age, the opportunity to excel at the university level. The average entering age is currently 13.5 years and all EEP students must be under the age of 16 by June 1st of the year in which they apply. (Early Entrance Program, 2004, ¶ 1)

In order to create a "home base" for EEP students, the program administrators and staff have their offices located in close proximity to the EEP student lounge, kitchen, computer room, study room, and social area. Sensitive to the developmental needs of the young students, the staff is always available for support, guidance, and counseling, and they have made every effort to foster an atmosphere that resembles a high school in the most positive sense (even though the coursework is all college level):

> Each entering freshman class has a common Schedule of Curriculum including classes designed to simulate a normal secondary school curriculum. These classes include Science, History, English and Mathematics. EEP students must be on campus at least 4 days per week, and are encouraged to maintain a presence in the EEP Lounge to facilitate the development of friendships and inclusion in campus events and activities. The students in the EEP are also encouraged to maintain the relationships they formed with their friends from their previous schools and often participate in their traditional school activities. Such normal activities include sports, dances and, of course, the prom. In addition to EEP, CSULA also houses the Los Angeles County High School for the Arts (LACHSA), which has a population of 500 adolescent high school students. While these students do not take classes with the EEP students, we encourage interaction between

these two groups of highly talented young students. This presence of a normalized high school population on the campus allows the EEP students to blend in and go relatively unnoticed by the normal aged undergraduate students. (Early Entrance Program, 2004, ¶ 4)

In order to ensure that the fit between a student and the program is appropriate, the EEP usually requires students to take a minimum of two courses (eight units) during the summer prior to their entry into college. This is referred to as the Provisional Summer Quarter. In order to become a fully matriculated college student, a student must earn a 3.0 GPA and receive passing grades on all assignments during the provisional period. Once admitted, EEP participants are expected to remain at CSULA for the duration of their undergraduate education, which typically is 4–5 years.

Admissions Criteria

Applicants must provide evidence of outstanding achievement and perform at the very top ranges on standardized tests. Applicants should perform "at a level indicating a readiness for college level work on the Washington Pre-College Test and University entrance exams for specific disciplines." (Early Entrance Program, 2004, ¶ 6)

Comments of Mr. Richard Maddox, Director of EEP at California State University Los Angeles

1. What makes your early entrance program unique?

The age of entrants ranges typically between 11 and 15.9 years of age, but students as young as 9 have been admitted. We have [more than] 150 students in full-time attendance; students are admitted as full-time students immediately following their provisional assessment period. EEPsters are extraordinarily involved in campus life including involvement in programs, clubs, events, student governance, and social activities. Research opportunities are available for our students in all major academic disciplines and EEPsters are highly involved with faculty projects and are awarded numerous prestigious scholarships including (since 1995) six national Phi Kappa Phi graduate fellowships. Each fall, a new cohort of freshmen begin the EEP Freshmen Curriculum that includes GE courses in English, mathematics, history, and science. Each spring a new class of EEP graduates earns the bachelor's degree en route to continuing their education at some of the finest graduate programs in the nation. I am very proud to say that the EEP at CSULA, which I have worked to develop, is truly becoming a national model for radical acceleration efforts.

2. For whom is the EEP ideal? For whom is it not?

The EEP is ideal for students between 13 and 14 years of age who are highly gifted and are relatively unhappy with the pace, structure, and curriculum of traditional school. We evaluate three main criteria in terms of admission that include need, motivation, and readiness. In addition, we also assess character, history of academic achievement, parent support, and potential contribution to the program and the university.

The EEP is not appropriate for students who are otherwise happy and adjusted with the academics and environment of normal school. In other words, if a highly gifted and talented student is content with traditional school, why would [he or she] want or need to leave?

3. Obviously, you select students for the EEP with the expectation that they will succeed. What is your definition of success?

Academically speaking, [success is earning] a 3.0 GPA and above. In less scholastic terms we would consider a student to be successful if [he or she is] socially adjusted, personally happy, from a warm and supportive home environment, and involved with friends and extracurricular activities in school.

117

4. Based on your observations and experience, what personal characteristics/qualities (e.g., ability to focus) seem to help students succeed as early entrants?

Self-discipline, self-regulatory behaviors, self-management skills, a motivation to excel, and dedication to scholarship help students succeed. Also, strong writers are especially successful, as are those with good verbal communication skills. Students who are outgoing, personable, and who have positive personalities are also usually more successful in school.

5. In your view, what personal factors or characteristics/qualities (e.g., poor study habits) hinder early entrants from succeeding in college?

A lack of discipline, poor focus, an underdeveloped work ethic, minimal dedication to scholarship, and most importantly, disruptive or otherwise negative and dysfunctional families may lead a student to a less than successful school career.

6. What external/environmental factors (e.g., supportive family) seem to promote success among the EEP students?

Supportive, caring, and educated parents are usually those we associate with successful students.

7. What external/environmental factors (e.g., distractions in residence hall) hinder success among the EEP students?

"Pushy" or overbearing and demanding parents who are trying to live vicariously through the student are often associated with less than successful students. Also, distance from campus has had a negative effect on some students, as they must be on campus on a regular basis. The travel time takes a toll on the entire family.

Georgia Academy of Mathematics, Engineering, & Science (GAMES)

Another early entrance program in Georgia is housed in Middle Georgia College, a 2-year institution that is part of the University System of Georgia. Located in Cochran, GA, GAMES offers high school juniors and seniors the chance to complete high school and earn an associate's degree in math or science concurrently. (Younger students with remarkable ability may be considered for admission.) Students who want to major in engineering should be aware that they will not be awarded an associate's degree after completing 2 years of coursework, but have the option of: (a) completing their coursework at a 4-year institution that offers an engineering program without earning an associate's degree, or (b) earning an associate's degree in a field of math or science at Middle Georgia College before transferring to a university and declaring a major in engineering. All courses taken by GAMES students are college-level and fulfill the requirements for high school graduation, assuming the student is a resident of Georgia.

In addition to college-level coursework, GAMES students enjoy other benefits such as GAMES-sponsored activities/workshops (e.g., special field trips; workshops on study skills, time management, and test-taking skills) and participation in student organizations and clubs on campus. One potential drawback is that these students are not permitted to participate in varsity sports (a drawback that most early entrants will encounter wherever they attend college). They reside in Grace Hall, a dormitory reserved exclusively for GAMES students and are supervised by a live-in dorm mother, a live-in activities director, and resident advisors.

Two explicit goals of GAMES are to nurture the talent of their students and to encourage these talented individuals to stay in Georgia:

> The end result of the GAMES program is to keep the best minds of math, engineering, and science in

Georgia. With the increasing demand for scientific and technological expertise, Academy graduates will significantly influence and contribute to the development of business, industry, education, and research in Georgia. Developing our best minds and talents through this program can help make Georgia more competitive with other states and the United States more competitive with other nations. (Georgia Academy of Mathematics, Engineering, & Science, 2006, ¶ 6)

Admission Criteria

Applicants are expected to have a high school GPA of 3.5 or better and a combined score of at least 1100 on the SAT-I (Minimums of 560 Math and 530 Verbal) or a Composite score of 24 on the ACT (Minimums of 24 Math and 23 Verbal). For more information about the application process, visit http://www.mgc.edu/academic/scimathbus/games.

Comments by Ms. Lisa Whitaker, Director of GAMES

1. What makes your early entrance program unique?

GAMES students receive an associate's degree from Middle Georgia College and a high school diploma from their high school.

2. For whom is GAMES ideal? For whom is it not?

[Being] an academic scholar is important, but not inclusive. A student must be self-motivated and disciplined to perform at this level at this young age.

3. Obviously, you select students for GAMES with the expectation that they will succeed. What is your definition of success?

The ability to proceed to the next level (a 4-year institution in this case) with the knowledge and skills to excel.

4. Based on your observations and experience, what personal characteristics/qualities (e.g., ability to focus) seem to help students succeed as early entrants?

They must be highly motivated and mature, and have outstanding time management skills and good study skills.

5. In your view, what personal factors or characteristics/qualities (e.g., poor study habits) hinder early entrants from succeeding in college?

Immaturity, poor time management, and keeping the same study habits used at the high school level.

6. What external/environmental factors (e.g., supportive family) seem to promote success among the GAMES students?

The competitiveness of peers, family support, having friends watching to see "if they'll make it," and the ridicule factor (of high school) being removed; it's OK to be smart!

7. What external/environmental factors (e.g., distractions in residence hall) hinder success among the GAMES students?

The social atmosphere, especially for those who have never had a social life, and for some, the lack of a present authority figure.

National Academy of Arts, Sciences, and Engineering (NAASE)

Designed to work in concert with The University of Iowa (UI) Honors Program, the National Academy of Arts, Sciences, and Engineering was established to facilitate the intellectual and educational development of highly able students who are ready for college one year early. They must also be attracted to the idea of attending The University of Iowa, a leading research institution with approximately 100 different major and minor areas of study and certificate programs. In contrast to some early entrance programs that focus exclusively on mathematics, science, and the technological fields, NAASE welcomes students to pursue educational degrees in the humanities and arts, as well. Those who are considering applying to NAASE must be aware that the program is not designed for students who hope to transfer after a year or two to another institution. NAASE students are expected to complete their undergraduate programs at UI. Merit- and need-based scholarships are available. For inquiries about financial assistance, visit http://www.education.uiowa.edu/belinblank/programs/naase or contact the program directly (see appendix).

Once admitted to NAASE, the students receive academic, social, and emotional support from program staff as they navigate their way through their first year of college. Although the intensity of support tends to decrease as NAASE students find their way and become more adjusted to college life, the staff is available to them throughout their years at UI. NAASE provides its students with cultural and social activities to supplement the wide array of opportunities that are available to them through the university.

The Belin-Blank Center and Honors Program recently acquired their own building, the Blank Honors Center, which is located next to Daum Residence Hall, where NAASE students, UI Honors Program students, and other Belin-Blank Center university program students reside. Students can access the Blank Honors Center via a skywalk, conveniently taking advantage of the center's amenities.

Admissions Criteria

It is recommended that NAASE applicants have a composite score on a standardized test (e.g., SAT, or ACT) at or above the national 95th percentile and a high school GPA of at least 3.5. For more information, visit http://www.education.uiowa.edu/belinblank/programs/naase.

Comments of Dr. Nicholas Colangelo, Director, and Dr. Susan Assouline, Associate Director, Connie Belin and Jacqueline N. Blank International Center for Gifted Education and Talent Development (Belin-Blank Center) and NAASE

1. What makes your early entrance program unique?

NC: It is national. Students can leave high school after their junior year. We put considerable thought and effort into including the parents in the process, as well as a comprehensive look at the students.

SA: Students are encouraged to have "completed" as much high school coursework as possible. Students are encouraged to bring closure to their high school experience by graduating, if they desire, attending prom, etc. We do not encourage transferring to another school once they have entered Iowa. They sometimes do so, but we do not actively promote this—this is in contrast to TAMS, for example.

2. For whom is NAASE ideal? For whom is it not?

NC: Ideal students are those who are ready for more challenge in their lives. They are ready both cognitively and socially/emotionally. NAASE is not ideal for students who just "want to get away from high school."

SA: NAASE is ideal really for just about anybody who is ready for university coursework and life at a public Research I institution. Students from large schools with lots of AP courses will thrive, as well as students from rural settings where there is no one who has the same level of ability and achievement.

3. Obviously, you select students for NAASE with the expectation that they will succeed. What is your definition of success?

NC: Success is doing well academically. Successful students are the type of students who should be on a Dean's

123

List. Students should also feel excitement and fulfillment for the university experience.

SA: Graduating in 4 years or fewer with a GPA of 3.0 or higher and a minimal degree of stress with a maximum level of participation in extracurriculars, for example, clubs, organizations, music, and drama.

4. Based on your observations and experience, what personal characteristics/qualities (e.g., ability to focus) seem to help students succeed as early entrants?

NC: They must be willing to study more than they did in high school. They should have flexibility with a new environment and not be discouraged by minor setbacks.

SA: Not having a relationship issue that they left behind (with family or friends), good study skills, and No. 1—attendance in class. If a student attends, they are halfway on the road to success. The ability to be flexible in the issues related to dorm life is also helpful.

5. In your view, what personal factors or characteristics/qualities (e.g., poor study habits) hinder early entrants from succeeding in college?

NC: Poor study habits will be a problem. Lack of willingness to share with staff may be problematic, and other difficulties may be encountered—sometimes, financial issues.

SA: Poor class attendance, poor study habits, time management and organizational skills, substance use or abuse, and difficulty with relationships hinder success.

6. What external/environmental factors (e.g., supportive family) seem to promote success among the NAASE students?

NC: NAASE students and staff, parents/family support, and understanding faculty members.

SA: Whatever can be done to relieve the students from stress (financial, relationships, etc.).

7. What external/environmental factors (e.g., distractions in residence hall) hinder success among the NAASE students?

NC: Poor roommate fit, and boyfriend/girlfriend problems either back at high school or at the university.

SA: Mainly difficulties with roommates.

Program for the Exceptionally Gifted (PEG)

PEG is an early college entrance program located on the campus of Mary Baldwin College (MBC) in Staunton, VA, that is designed specifically for academically talented young women who may apply during or after their eighth-grade year. In order to ensure that PEG students do not have gaps in their knowledge due to their radical acceleration, the program has established course requirements that PEG students must fulfill that may exceed MBC general education requirements.

Students who enter PEG as rising 9th or 10th graders are called "Alphas" and reside in a special dormitory until they have completed their sophomore year. PEG students receive a great deal of personalized attention. Aside from around-the-clock supervision in the residence hall, they meet on a regular basis with PEG staff to discuss academic and/or personal concerns. When students have doctor or dental appointments or errands to run off campus, PEG staff provides transportation and accompanies them. In addition, the staff organizes leisure activities on campus, as well as off campus:

Every weekend, PEG staff members arrange recreation on or off campus. PEG excursions include the Richmond Science Museum, the Virginia State Fair, Washington, D.C., Virginia Beach, and King's Dominion. PEG students go to dances at local pri-

125

vate schools. Students see movies and the opera. They make and paint pottery. They go camping, ice skating, roller-skating, snow tubing, and skiing. Activities are varied to accommodate the wide variety of interests of our students. (Program for the Exceptionally Gifted, n.d.b, ¶ 6)

PEG students are eligible for a number of scholarships, which are based on various criteria, for example, academic performance, minority status, and/or major area of study. Visit http://www.mbc.edu/peg for details about available funding.

Admissions Criteria

Applicants who are given serious consideration for PEG must have a strong academic record. In addition to excellent grades, "achievement test scores must be in the 90th percentiles [and applicants must] have SAT or ACT scores comparable to those of entering college freshmen" (Program for the Exceptionally Gifted, n.d.a, ¶ 2).

Comments of Dr. Elizabeth Connell, Director of PEG

I. What makes your early entrance program unique?

The Program for the Exceptionally Gifted (PEG), now in its 22nd year, remains the only early entrance program that accepts gifted girls as young as 12 or 13 to live on a college campus with other gifted students in a self-contained and fully supervised residence hall. PEG is a program that focuses on the full development of gifted females at a liberal arts college where faculty and staff are committed to the higher education and development of women. PEG students are enrolled in regular college courses with traditional-aged Mary Baldwin College students and adult degree students and participate fully in all campus organizations, teams, and leadership positions. In addition to an exciting academic challenge, PEG provides the underage student with true peers and a residential program that offers support, enrichment, and structure in an age-appropriate manner.

2. For whom is PEG ideal? For whom is it not?

PEG is ideal for students who seek both the personal and academic challenges that such radical acceleration can provide and who possess the maturity and independence to pursue college-level work in a residential setting.

PEG is not ideal for students who lack the intellectual capacity and emotional maturity to succeed in a college environment away from home.

3. Obviously, you select students for PEG with the expectation that they will succeed. What is your definition of success?

Successful PEG students are motivated to learn new things and to do their best. They are not afraid to take risks and try new things and they learn and grow from their mistakes. They look for ways to use their gifts and talents to serve others and make a difference in the world.

4. Based on your observations and experience, what personal characteristics/qualities (e.g., ability to focus) seem to help students succeed as early entrants?

The personal characteristics of curiosity and perseverance are most helpful for success at PEG. The intrepid academic explorer who values learning and wants it to be fun and interesting is the student who will be most successful as an early college entrant at PEG.

5. In your view, what personal factors or characteristics/qualities (e.g., poor study habits) hinder early entrants from succeeding in college?

127

Students who are less successful at PEG are those who entered for the wrong reasons. They came because they felt pressure to rush through school by family members or friends, not because they felt a personal desire for intellectual challenge and growth.

6. What external/environmental factors (e.g., supportive family) seem to promote success among the PEG students?

The family who gets satisfaction from supporting and affirming their daughter's interests and abilities for her own sake and not for any future benefit promote the greatest success at PEG.

7.What external/environmental factors (e.g., distractions in the residence hall) hinder success among the PEG students?

Parents who are unwilling to let their daughter make mistakes and learn from them and to develop independence hinder success more than any other environmental factor at PEG. Parents who encourage their daughter to identify, own, and then solve [her] own problems are most effective and helpful.

Resident Honors Program (RHP)

RHP is a residential early entrance program located on the campus of the University of Southern California (USC) in Los Angeles, that admits 30 qualified students per year to college one year early. An exciting feature of the program that affords its early entrants a comprehensive learning experience is the Thematic Option Honors Program.

> Thematic Option Core courses break down boundaries which separate disciplines and teach students to appreciate the relationships between literature, history, philosophy and science. The core curriculum is built around small courses, taught by many of the University's finest faculty, and writing classes, which include biweekly, one-on-one tutorials. (Resident Honors Program, n.d., ¶ 3)

RHP students are strongly encouraged to take advantage of the plethora of academic resources that USC has to offer. Considering USC has more than 100 degree programs (undergraduate, graduate, and professional) and is a well-respected private research university, RHP students have seemingly countless opportunities to find their passions and develop their interests, whatever they may be. With the assistance of their advisors, RHP students are allowed to put together individualized programs of study, which gives them even more flexibility.

Given the vast number of social and cultural activities that are available to USC students, those participating in RHP are expected to become integrated into the larger USC community. Although some activities are scheduled exclusively for RHP students and although RHP students reside together in a special residence hall (two practices aimed to help build cohesion among the students), the program is designed to ultimately help the students branch out and find their niche outside of the program.

In contrast to some programs that help their students to transfer to other institutions after a year or two, RHP holds the expectation that its students will complete their undergraduate degrees at USC. RHP offers substantial monetary awards and scholarships to many of its students. Visit the RHP Web site (http://www.usc.edu/dept/LAS/general_studies/RHP) or contact the program (see appendix for contact information) for further details.

Admissions Criteria

Strong candidates for RHP are those who have at least an A- average and have completed AP or IB courses. The new SAT minimum score requirement is 2050 combined, and the minimum composite ACT score is 32. Applicants also must demonstrate strong writing skills on a standardized writing examination (the SAT-II writing score or ACT writing section score). Average class scores have been above 1470 on the old SAT and 33 on the ACT. Average GPAs have been 4.0.

Comments of Dr. Pennelope Von Helmolt,
Director of RHP

1. What makes your early entrance program unique?

The most unique aspect of the Resident Honors Program (RHP) is the students themselves. They are an eclectic academic, social, and geographic mix, and every class has its own unique personality.

Another unique feature is that our students do not participate in any kind of bridging program or special curriculum. When they are admitted into RHP, they are considered fullfledged freshmen and are given the same opportunities as any other typical freshman.

RHP also affords our students the rare opportunity of extremely personalized attention within the context of a large research university. We typically have between 20 and 25 RHP students matriculating in the university in any given freshman class, and the group's modest size enables the program administrators to get to know the students and what they want out of college. Thus, we are better able to help them achieve their goals.

RHP, unlike some early entrance programs, is geared specifically towards high school juniors. We only admit students who will have completed their junior year the spring before entrance into USC. We do not admit students who have completed high school early or who are extremely talented but have yet to complete their junior year.

Another way in which the program is unique is that it is tied into USC's Thematic Option (TO) program, our interdisciplinary honors general education program. Nearly all of the entering RHP students participate in TO, and this is another way to give the students a nurturing intellectual community that still offers the resources of a larger school.

Additionally, we offer opportunities for faculty mentoring and special programming for the students, both academic and social, so that these exceptionally bright students can form their own bonds that hopefully will last far beyond college.

2. For whom is RHP ideal? For whom is it not?

RHP is ideal for the young, the smart, and the restless. The students in our program are in a hurry to move beyond the coursework at their high schools. They want a new challenge and are socially and emotionally ready to take the next step to college. The ideal RHP candidate is a superb student, has very strong test scores, and possesses a strong résumé that demonstrates a readiness for the rigors of college coursework. Often times, these students have extraordinary leadership potential and a burgeoning curiosity to explore and seek out new knowledge.

RHP is not ideal for students who do not possess the high level of maturity required of a student entering college. The students who do not benefit from RHP are those that, instead of wanting to move ahead in their field or in their academic studies, simply want to get out of school (high school, college, and beyond) as quickly as possible. All the RHP students are in a hurry, but those that do not have the fervor to learn do not find RHP to be the environment for which they are looking. Additionally, RHP is not a program for all precocious youth; we do not accept students who have not completed their junior year of high school before entrance in the fall.

3. Obviously, you select students for RHP with the expectation that they will succeed. What is your definition of success?

I am struck by how our students unexpectedly redefine conventional notions of success, so this is a difficult question to answer. However, the "success" of a student can in part be measured by how well he or she integrates into the USC community—participating in clubs, leading activities, attending office hours, doing well in [his or her] courses, etc. We think it is important that our students integrate into the general freshman population so that no one even realizes that they are a special, younger population.

As they move on in their college careers, we expect the RHP students to assume leadership roles throughout the USC community, develop a love of academia, and look to pursue

131

postgraduate studies. Alternatively, if graduate studies are not a student's desired path, we hope that the RHP students develop a cosmopolitan sensibility. That is, we want them to travel, explore and encounter new people and places, and incorporate that knowledge into their lives.

4. Based on your observations and experience, what personal characteristics/qualities (e.g., ability to focus) seem to help students succeed as early entrants?

The quality that suggests a student will succeed in RHP is, above all, an overriding drive to learn and broaden his or her horizons. They are students who approach every opportunity and every challenge with a love of life and a spirit of adventure. They approach most endeavors enthusiastically and with an eye for learning something new.

Time management skills are imperative for success. A successful student also displays a willingness to seek help when necessary, be it academic help from a professor, personal help from a fellow student or RA, or administrative help from the RHP staff. These are the students [who] enrich their lives and their experiences here at USC.

Additionally, a high level of maturity is an important factor of a student's success. We measure a student's maturity in terms of his or her ability to communicate ideas to others; strong writing skills; and an enjoyment of reading, investigating, encountering, and discovering new realms of knowledge on his or her own terms.

5. In your view, what personal factors or characteristics/qualities (e.g., poor study habits) hinder early entrants from succeeding in college?

Poor time management and chronic procrastination are extreme hindrances to success in college. Immaturity is another; this can be evidenced by poor or absent interaction with one's peers or professors, oversleeping, and failure to attend class.

6. What external/environmental factors (e.g., supportive family) seem to promote success among the RHP students?

The support of the family and the RHP community promotes the success of the students in RHP. Most importantly, though, is the family's support of the student's decision to enter college a year early. Additionally, the family's encouragement of the student no matter the major or course of study that [he or she] choose[s] is another important element of success. Students who feel extreme pressure from their family to follow a certain course are liable to lose the drive to succeed.

Faculty mentors are another major influence on a student's success. A new set of interesting and similarly driven and intelligent friends also promotes a collaborative and invigorating passion to succeed academically.

Although it is not required, we try to house RHP students together in one of two residence halls so that they can bond and help each other with academic and personal issues.

7. What external/environmental factors (e.g., distractions in the residence hall) hinder success among the RHP students?

Some of the external hindrances include: taking advantage of too many of USC's myriad programs at the expense of studying; pressure from other students to participate in activities when a student needs to study; and parents pressuring their child to follow a course of study in which he or she is not interested, which often takes the form of parents pressuring their child to think about academics solely in terms of a career path. Additionally, some of our local students find it difficult to integrate into the USC community when their family requires them to commute home every weekend.

133

Simon's Rock College of Bard (SRC)

Great Barrington, MA, is the home of Simon's Rock College, which has the distinction of being the nation's only

4-year liberal arts and sciences college specifically designed for younger students. Students may elect to earn either an associate's degree or bachelor's degree from SRC and may be able to arrange getting their high school diplomas and graduating with their high school classes. Of course, this is contingent on the cooperation of the students' high schools. Many SRC students do not obtain diplomas or test for the General Educational Diploma (GED).

In addition to providing students with ample opportunities to pursue their own academic interests, Simon's Rock implements a rigorous required liberal arts and science curriculum, with an emphasis on developing students' writing skills. Typically, SRC students truncate their high school experience by 1 or 2 years in exchange for an opportunity to learn in an environment that embraces intellectual curiosity. As stated so eloquently on the college's Web site:

> The program is designed to engage students in the life of the mind by making them aware of both the Western cultural heritage and modes of thought from other cultures, introducing them to the spectrum of thought in the liberal arts and sciences, developing their intellectual curiosity, and empowering them to satisfy that curiosity by thinking and learning independently. At Simon's Rock, students are also encouraged to test theory in practice—in the laboratory, the studio, and the field, in rehearsal and performance—to develop a sense of themselves as thinkers and creators with individual voices and perspectives. (Simon's Rock College of Bard, 2006a, ¶ 2)

Simon's Rock students appear to have plentiful opportunities to expand their awareness of different cultures. The college offers travel abroad experiences and encourages students to attend cultural events within the vicinity of the campus. These include musical, dance, and theatrical performances; art exhibits; poetry readings; lectures; film series; and other events in Berkshire County. To compliment the social and cultural activities at Simon's Rock, the college has developed the Recreational Athletic Program (RAP), which provides students with opportunities to participate in both noncompetitive and competitive athletics.

Because the entire college is dedicated to serving the unique developmental needs of young entrants, a strong support network is available to students:

> We have a strong, carefully planned support system made up of older students, faculty, staff and advisors who pay attention to each student and help make the transition to college as smooth as possible. New student housing is single sex and supervised by adult residence directors. A spirit of camaraderie characterizes the campus, so that people pay attention to how others are doing. The 9:1 student-faculty ratio ensures individual attention to each student from faculty members expert both in their fields and in helping students to face the challenge of beginning college early. (Simon's Rock College of Bard, 2006b, ¶ 8)

A considerable amount of financial assistance is offered to Simon's Rock students. Approximately 80% of them receive scholarships of varying amounts. The Acceleration to Excellence Program (AEP) offers a full merit scholarship for the 2-year Associate of Arts degree program to approximately 20 students per year. The AEP also offers up to 30 partial scholarships. Many students also rely on need-based aid and/or loans to finance their educations at Simon's Rock.

Admissions Criteria

No minimum requirements for standardized test scores are stated on the Simon's Rock Web site or application; however, students should have a strong academic record. Applicants who have less than exemplary grades may be considered yet they, like all applicants, must demonstrate intelligence, a love for learning, independent thinking, and a solid

135

work ethic. Simon's Rock takes a holistic approach to student selection.

Comments of Dr. Mary Marcy, Vice President and Provost, Simon's Rock College

1. What makes your early entrance program unique?

Simon's Rock College is the nation's only 4-year institution dedicated exclusively to the education of the younger scholar. Our mission is entirely early college, and we aim to provide the highest quality liberal arts college education to students at an earlier age than the traditional institution of higher education. We are not co-located with another college, but are a 240-acre residential campus serving only early college students. This means that our curricular offerings are as rigorous as any college in the nation, and our residential and co-curricular systems are designed for younger students. Faculty advising is an essential relationship for students, who meet once a week with their advisor. Classroom instruction takes place in small seminar style with [a] faculty/student ratio of 9:1. Simon's Rock recognizes that students' intellectual development and social/emotional development may occur at different rates, and we work to provide challenge and support appropriate for all areas of students' needs.

2. For whom is Simon's Rock College ideal? For whom is it not?

Simon's Rock is ideal for students who are bright, motivated, and ready for the social and intellectual challenges of college work. We accept students who excel academically and are not adequately challenged by their current high school or educational environment. We also accept students who may not have exceptional academic standing but are not happy with the high school experience for any variety of reasons. Students who are not motivated or who are uncomfortable having relationships with adults will not do well at Simon's Rock, as it is a challenging and highly personal environment. Students who are motivated and able will find that it is a supportive but rigorous learning community designed to nurture their growth personally and intellectually.

3. Obviously, you select students for Simon's Rock with the expectation that they will succeed. What is your definition of success?

The most immediate definition of success is progress toward and ultimate completion of a degree program. [More than] 85% of entering students receive the A.A. degree after 2 years, and most students also complete a bachelor's degree at either Simon's Rock or transfer [to] institutions that regularly include Stanford, the University of Chicago, Brown University, and others. Students who do not complete their degrees at Simon's Rock College because they choose to transfer early to 4-year or graduate programs offering specialized degrees and who do well in those programs are considered successful by Simon's Rock College standards.

4. Based on your observations and experience, what personal characteristics/qualities (e.g., ability to focus) seem to help students succeed as early entrants?

Simon's Rock College students possess a wide range of skills and personal attributes [that] contribute to their success. Intellectual curiosity and an interest in world affairs are common characteristics among Simon's Rock students. They often are creative, adventurous, and willing to take risks to accomplish their goals. Simon's Rock students tend to be independent thinkers. Students who question authority and doubt common schools of thought perform well. Taking personal initiative and caring about making a difference in the world is another quality that students share. Students who see themselves within a larger context and take responsibility for their learning because they have a desire to be smart and to succeed usually do well at Simon's Rock College and after they graduate.

5. In your view, what personal factors or characteristics/qualities (e.g., poor study habits) hinder early entrants from succeeding in college?

A lack of motivation or self-discipline may hinder the success of students. Because Simon's Rock is a close learning community, students who are uncomfortable engaging in intellectual discussions, expressing their ideas, and considering ideas that may challenge their own may find it difficult to succeed. Students without an interest in overcoming obstacles that they may face during their academic careers may have difficulty with the rigorous demands of their studies.

6. What external/environmental factors (e.g., supportive family) seem to promote success among the Simon's Rock students?

Having a supportive family with high aspirations for their success aids in students' determination to do well in their academic work. The college has created a similar supportive structure with a faculty whose commitments to seeing their students succeed far surpasses that at other colleges. A small student/faculty ratio contributes to a personalized learning environment and enables faculty to closely observe and support students' progress in their work. A notable characteristic of the learning environment is the high level of respect given to the intellects of young scholars. Their ideas are taken seriously and they are treated as intellectual equals in the classroom. Similarly, faculty regularly teach outside of their own disciplines, which provides a model for students who see their professors learning new material along with their students.

7. What external/environmental factors (e.g., distractions in residence hall) hinder success among the Simon's Rock students?

There are few obstacles within the supportive community that exist at the college. Students who might have had a poor academic preparation but by other standards have qualified for entrance may find the academic work difficult and, without adequate focus, might not succeed. Financial means may sometimes be an obstacle, although scholarships are available to help students with lesser means.

Texas Academy of Mathematics and Science (TAMS)

Since its inception in 1987, TAMS, located at the University of North Texas (UNT), has been serving academically talented students from across the state of Texas who are ready for the challenge of college after their sophomore year of high school. Despite the limitation that it is an option for Texas residents only, TAMS is one of the largest early entrance programs in that it admits approximately 200 students per year. Consequently, TAMS students, who are referred to as TAMSters, have a large pool of age-mates from which to establish friendships and find their social niche. Another implication of TAMS' impressive size is its capacity to sponsor many social and extracurricular opportunities within the program. These opportunities are in addition to the ones offered to all UNT students, in which TAMSters are encouraged to participate. According to the TAMS Web site,

> Some 20 TAMS organizations offer numerous leadership and service opportunities, from Key Club, Jets, and Student Council, to musical and theatrical groups and intramural athletics. The Academy sponsors dances, game and activity nights, movies, plays, and recreation, with the prom an annual highlight. TAMSters also participate in over 350 UNT sponsored organizations and events. (Texas Academy of Mathematics and Science, n.d.a, ¶ 3)

With this introduction, one might be mislead to believe that the highlight of TAMS is its broad array of social and extracurricular offerings. In actuality, the hallmark of the program is its academic rigor:

> The goal of the TAMS experience is to develop the whole person—but the focus of the experience is in the academic program. Rigorous university courses, participation in seminal research projects and in scientific laboratories engaged in cutting edge research, opportunities to engage in artistic and musical pursuits, in reflective philosophical discourses, and in exercise to enhance physical and mental well-being are all part of this academic focus and the Academy experience. (Texas Academy of Mathematics and Science, n.d.b, ¶ 1)

At the end of 2 years, after having earned 57 semester credits, TAMS students receive an advanced high school diploma with transferable college credit and make the choice to finish their undergraduate degrees at UNT or transfer to another university.

Like other formal early entrance programs, TAMS provides its students with academic and social/emotional support. In addition to academic counselors, TAMS has a staff psychologist who specializes in adolescent development and can assist TAMSters with any difficulties related to their adjustment to college. TAMS also provides free tutoring and workshops aimed at improving students' study skills, note taking, time management, and the like. Students reside in McConnell Hall, which is well supervised by 2 full-time hall directors, 14 resident advisors, and 4 program advisors who are trained to understand the needs of early entrants.

Admission Criteria

Given the program's strong emphasis on mathematics, the following courses must be successfully completed by the end of an applicant's 10th-grade year: Geometry, Algebra I, and Algebra II. TAMS also requires that students' SAT scores be competitive with traditional college-bound students who want to major in math or science.

Comments of Dr. Richard. J. Sinclair, Dean, and Dr. Donna Fleming, Director of Counseling, TAMS

I. What makes your early entrance program unique?

RS: TAMS is a residential program on a major university campus. [Students take] all college courses (57 semester credit hours) to earn a high school diploma. It has a strong focus on student research, [and students have] the ability to win high school honors (Intel, Siemens, etc.), as well as college honors (Goldwater, Udall, etc.). TAMS allows [students to earn a] college degree in 2 years after [completing the] TAMS [program].

DF: TAMS offers the college academic experience simultaneously with age-appropriate social opportunities with adult support and guidance. Therefore, while enrolled in an all-college curriculum taught by college faculty, students do not have to sacrifice the valuable experiences that traditional high school clubs, organizations, programs, and peer relationships provide. In addition, TAMS has policies implemented by its own administration and staff to ensure that the students' environment is safe and supportive.

2. For whom is TAMS ideal? For whom is it not?

RS: TAMS is ideal for a student who cannot find intellectual challenge in high school, needs a true intellectual peer group, has an interest in research, and is motivated to accelerate his or her college education. TAMS is ideal for girls ... no intellectual stigma.

TAMS is not a good choice for gifted underachievers. Students must be very self-motivated and mature. They must have very strong math skills despite career direction. The academic demands are very high. The program is not individualized.

DF: TAMS is ideal for students who have a history of excelling above their peers in academics, achievement motivation, love of learning, resiliency, independence, and maturity. It is also very helpful if they have a vision for what they want to achieve in the future in the way of educational degree programs and careers.

TAMS is not ideal for students who need the structure of the high school curriculum, pressure from parents and/or teachers to perform to expectations, frequent supervision and guidance in making appropriate decisions, and who are lacking in focus toward their future goals.

3. Obviously, you select students for TAMS with the expectation that they will succeed. What is your definition of success?

RS: My minimal expectation is a 3.0 GPA and completion of program requirements. "Success" is clear personal growth, exploration, participation, and achievement beyond the minimum required. So many options exist that an individual's success is hard to define. The program provides endless opportunity. Exploring those positive opportunities is "success."

DF: I define success for TAMS students as multidimensional. Academically, success is defined as a very good grade point average, but not necessarily a 4.0. I would hope that successful students would excel in the core curriculum, but also challenge themselves by enrolling in stimulating elective courses and participating with faculty mentors in research. In the personal realm, success for TAMS students involves increasing confidence, resiliency when confronted with challenges/obstacles, a clearer understanding of personal strengths and weaknesses, a vision of how they want to live their lives in the future, and the development of skills that will enhance their abilities to establish fulfilling social lives and careers.

4. Based on your observations and experience, what personal characteristics/qualities (e.g., ability to focus) seem to help students succeed as early entrants?

RS: Most important is being a true high achiever with the determination to overcome obstacles, such as the adjustment to college classes. Then would be the natural ability to [manage one's time]. Maturity is critical.

DF: I've mentioned previously that students need strong achievement motivation, a love of learning, resiliency, maturity, and the ability to make good decisions independently. What I've observed is that not all students coming here have had to face significant challenges to really "test" themselves. Some of the most successful students I have known here have come from difficult situations, including having parents who moved from other countries and who sacrificed already established careers to live in the United States. These students have watched their families work very hard to provide for them and to restart their lives. Other challenges students might have faced include being raised in a single-parent home, having a chronically ill family member, or loss of a parent through death or divorce. Other personal qualities I have noticed could be described as a "moral compass," or an intrinsic belief system of what is the right way to live for oneself and for others.

5. In your view, what personal factors or characteristics/qualities (e.g., poor study habits) hinder early entrants from succeeding in college?

RS: None of them have study skills. The ability to adjust quickly to new things is very important. Students who insist on relying on high school habits (waiting until the last minute, reliance on "osmosis" to learn, etc.) suffer in our environment. I believe these are the same talented students who would fail in college anyway.

DF: Personal qualities that hinder early entrants in addition to those previously mentioned include a sense of entitlement to success and recognition. In addition, students who are prone to give up easily, who have extremely limited social skills, who are not motivated to seek out answers on their own, and who are very rigid in their belief systems are not likely to be successful here.

143

6. What external/environmental factors (e.g., supportive family) seem to promote success among the TAMS students?

DF: A supportive family that is encouraging, as well as nurturing, seems to promote success here. Being able to reconnect with family on our "closed weekends" is helpful, and we've noticed that students who are so far from home that weekend travel is prohibitive have more adjustment issues. Being able to connect early on with a few peers or establishing a positive support network among students is also important.

7. What external/environmental factors (e.g., distractions in residence hall) hinder success among the TAMS students?

DF: Parents who put pressure on students in a negative way (nonsupportive; not encouraging) and parents who are too disengaged are risk factors for our students. In addition, staying up late, too much time on computer activities, and serious boyfriend/girlfriend relationships are also distractions.

Conclusion

This chapter featured several of the nation's most prominent early entrance programs. My primary intention in including the unique perspectives of the program directors and administrators was to bring each of the programs to life. Without question, a great deal can be learned about a program by examining its leadership. Based on my interactions with these individuals while working on this book, I have come to believe that they feel deeply committed to their work with early entrants and bring to their jobs a wealth of knowledge and experience, not to mention their heart and soul. My hope is that even if you are not interested in attending a special program such as any of those described in this chapter or listed in the appendix, you will take to heart the thoughtful advice offered by the program administrators who have interacted with and observed early entrants for many years. In Chapter 7, suggestions will be made for those who prefer to enter college on their own, without the support of an early entrance program.

7

Entering College Early Independently

Focus Questions for Students:

- On as scale of 1 (*not important*) to 10 (*extremely important*), how much weight will the factor of *prestige* carry in choosing a college?

- How important do you think it is to your parents that you attend a prestigious academic institution?

- Which of the factors in choosing a college (that are presented in this chapter) are most important to you? Rank them in order of importance.

- Which of the factors do you suppose are most important to your parents and which ones are less critical to them? Rank them in order of importance.

- Discuss your responses to the four preceding questions with your parents.

Focus Questions for Parents:

- On as scale of 1 (*not important*) to 10 (*extremely important*), how much weight do you think *prestige* should carry in your child's college selection process?

- How important is your opinion regarding the importance of prestige to your child?

- Which of the factors in choosing a college (that are presented in this chapter) are most important to you? Rank them in order of importance.

Focus Questions for Parents, continued:
• Which of the factors do you suppose are most important to your child and which ones are less critical to him or her? Rank them in order of importance.
• Discuss your responses to the four preceding questions with your son or daughter.

Introduction

If you have decided to enter college early but a special program with a cohort of other early entrants does not seem appealing, many more options open up. That is the good news. So, what is the daunting news, you wonder? Many more options open up. That's right. It all depends on how you look at it. As you know, with more options come more questions, and with more questions confusion tends to ensue (well, at least it does for me); however, as I discussed previously, whether you find decision making relatively easy or difficult, having options definitely beats the alternative.

If you decide to forgo the option of entering a special program such as the ones described in Chapter 6 or those listed in the appendix, in many ways you are in the same boat as traditional students who must decide where to apply for college out of seemingly countless options. If you have your hopes set on selective colleges/universities, you will be competing against highly able students who are older than you by one or more years and who may have more academic, social, and extracurricular experience (although not necessarily more academic talent) than you. With that said, you should not abandon this path if you believe that this is your best option.

The Viewpoints of Admissions Deans/Directors

As a counselor at the Johns Hopkins Center for Talented Youth who works with the highest ability students—those who participate in the Study of Exceptional Talent (SET)—I can attest to the fact that my colleagues and I have known students who have entered college early on their own and successfully completed degrees at top universities. Before many of the early entrance programs were developed, Dr. Stanley assisted a number of exceptionally able students in entering Johns Hopkins at a relatively young age. They have since gone on to lead productive and happy lives. These examples illustrate the fact that it is possible for highly qualified students to enter selective universities on their own at a younger-than-typical age. If that is what you have in mind, I offer you this advice: Make sure that you are at least as academically prepared as others in the applicant pool, that is, be sure that you can convince admissions committees that you are just as qualified for admission, if not more so, as older applicants. In addition to academic preparedness, it is imperative that you are socially and emotionally mature enough to handle the demands of college at a younger age. To substantiate this point, I will offer the viewpoints of a director and dean of admissions of two top-tier universities.

According to Dr. Marilyn McGrath Lewis, the director of Harvard College admissions, "We have similar expectations for applicants of any chronological age, including an expectation of personal maturity." She added that in instances in which younger applicants have not completed their high school programs, "we would wish to understand the specific reasons behind the decision to accelerate." When asked to comment on any concerns she and her staff would have about admitting a younger student, she remarked, "In every case, we are concerned to establish evidence of maturity and depth."

149

Dr. Carol Lunkenheimer, dean of undergraduate admissions at Northwestern University in Evanston, IL, remarked that

> Northwestern University normally will not admit a student who has not finished high school coursework. We have had very few 16-year-olds apply (I believe last year we had only three). We would not consider admitting a student much younger than that (e.g., 14 years old). Younger-than-typical applicants would have to be just as prepared as older applicants in order to be considered strong candidates. . . . If we had any concerns about an applicant, we would contact his or her guidance counselor to get a better sense of the student's maturity level. Often there is nothing to worry about. A lot of students have gone to boarding schools where they learned the practical and social skills to live on their own, which helps to prepare them for the residential part of the college experience.

These two examples serve to illustrate that selective institutions are called that for a reason—they can be choosy, and if they suspect an applicant has certain deficits (e.g., lack of maturity or depth) that would detract from the community they are forming, they may not be willing to take a chance on that individual. Older applicants who are suspected of having these deficits are also going to be under a great deal of scrutiny and will also be at a disadvantage, so the younger age in and of itself is not the issue. It is what often accompanies the younger age that may be problematic—a lower level of maturity (simply because one has not had as much time to mature) and gaps in knowledge relative to traditional applicants as a result of skipping high school content. Then, there is the issue of placing a younger student in a dormitory with older students. Each college or university may have its own policies regarding this matter.

Two Categories of Early Entrants

Individuals who enter college early simply because they have moved through the high school curriculum at an accelerated pace and have participated in extracurricular activities and volunteer work like their older counterparts are likely to be viewed in a different, more positive manner by admissions committees than applicants who have no intention to finish their high school programs before moving on to college and who consequently have gaps in their academic preparation. An important lesson that I have learned over the years, however, is to never say never. Despite our most educated guesses, my colleagues and I occasionally have been surprised by admissions decisions. Again, as I mentioned in a previous chapter, chance factors can have a major impact on outcomes. It is possible that, despite all of the cautions I have offered, a top-tier university may take a chance on a young applicant who does not appear to be as academically prepared as one might hope. Nevertheless, regardless of what decision an admissions committee reaches regarding an applicant, a prospective early entrant ultimately must pursue options that are conducive to his or her own growth and optimal development. Given his or her unique needs, these options may not necessarily include brand-name institutions that "look" impressive, yet may not be the ideal fit.

How It Looks Versus How It Is

Many academically talented students dream of attending schools like Harvard University and MIT (favorites among the families with whom I work). There are many other outstanding institutions of higher learning that consistently appear on these students' radar screens, as well—too many to mention here. I certainly will not argue that these learning environments are superb for some highly competitive, moti-

151

vated, and intelligent students. Perhaps one or more of them would be right for you. At the same time, there are excellent colleges and universities that may not have the name recognition of an Ivy League school, and therefore may not appear anywhere on high achievers' lists as a top choice, much less a safety school. However, these schools might serve an able student's needs quite well. Jay Mathews (2003), an education reporter and columnist for the *Washington Post* authored a book on this very topic entitled, *Harvard Schmarvard: Getting Beyond the Ivy League to the College That Is Best for You*. Like Mathews, I believe that there are many underappreciated colleges that could prove to be wonderful options for able students who are on the traditional educational trajectory (college after the senior year), as well as for those considering early entrance. So, what questions should one ask him- or herself in order to narrow down college choices?

Here We Go Again With the Questions!

The questions that must be answered at this point in the process will not lead you to narrow your options to a single institution, but they will help you to identify the factors that *should* carry more or less weight in your decision. Of course, the weight given to each of these factors will vary from person to person because what is important to one student may be less important or not important at all to another. An example that immediately comes to mind is of two early entrants I knew who attended the same high school prior to enrolling in an early entrance program. These students had drastically different reactions to the university's proximity to their hometown. One young woman felt devastated to be several hours away from home because she couldn't see her boyfriend on a regular basis. The other student did not mind the distance at all. The following questions are also pertinent to students who are entering a special program, not just for those who want to find a university or college on their own. Although the former group has relatively limited options (I estimate that at present, there are *at least* 17 well-recognized early college programs in the nation, including commuter and residential programs [see Tables 1 and 2 in Chapter 6]; however, it is likely that there may be other programs that are less well-known), those who are taking the independent route may have many more options. The following questions should be considered as you begin to think about your early entrance to college.

1 *How far away from home would you like to be?* If your response is, "I'd like to stay at home" your college options obviously are going to be constrained by geography, which is perfectly fine if that is what you want and need. As a commuter, you will need to work out the logistics of getting to and from college. This will probably involve your parents or guardians until you are of age to drive yourself. Public transportation may also be an option, depending on where you reside. If you plan to leave your hometown for college, it will be helpful for you to consider how often you expect to visit your family and friends. Making a trip home on an occasional weekend may be more feasible in terms of time and cost if you attend a college nearby or at least in the same region of the U.S. Others may be perfectly content attending a school across the U.S. or perhaps even abroad. My own research (Muratori, 2003; Muratori, Colangelo, & Assouline, 2003) has led me to believe that it is not necessarily the *actual* distance from home that matters as much as the *perceived* distance from home. A student who is 2 hours from home might experience more homesickness than one who moved across the nation to attend college. So, ask yourself, "How far is too far and how close is too close?" Regardless of your perception, choosing a college that is relatively close to home makes a lot of sense if you enter college at a particularly young age, because it will make it much easier for you to be involved in family events. Surely your parents (who may be responsible for your transportation for some time to come) will agree that the closer the proximity your school is to home, the more convenient it will be for them.

2 *How important is geographical location in your college selection?* A related question to the one above is whether there are certain regions of the U.S. to which you are most drawn. Factors other than how close or far away you want to be from home may affect your preferences. For instance, think about climate. Are there certain weather conditions that you would like to experience or avoid? (Prior to leaving Southern California, I admittedly thought questions about weather were superficial and irrelevant because there are no real weather changes in Southern California; however, after moving to the Midwest and then to the East Coast, I experienced "weather" for the first time and now understand how difficult it can be to adjust to different climates). You must remember that you are going to spend the next few years in college, so factors such as weather really can matter. For instance, some areas tend to get a lot of rain and/or may be cloudy and gray much of the time. This type of weather makes some people feel depressed, so spending several years in that environment would not be pleasant for them or even good for their health. In addition, are you more comfortable in an urban, rural, or suburban setting? What type of geographical environments will afford you the opportunity to do recreational and leisure activities that you enjoy? It is important to think beyond academics. This ties in to the next question.

3 *What are your extracurricular interests and which colleges have the resources to enable you to pursue your nonacademic interests?* One of the advantages of technology is that a person can easily obtain a wealth of information about virtually anything via the Internet. So, as you are gathering information about academic programs and financial aid on university Web sites, you should take the extra few moments to investigate university-sponsored social and extracurricular offerings and get information about the surrounding community. One caveat is that if you do enter college early, you will most likely be at a disadvan-

those who want to find a university or college on their own. Although the former group has relatively limited options (I estimate that at present, there are *at least* 17 well-recognized early college programs in the nation, including commuter and residential programs [see Tables 1 and 2 in Chapter 6]; however, it is likely that there may be other programs that are less well-known), those who are taking the independent route may have many more options. The following questions should be considered as you begin to think about your early entrance to college.

1 *How far away from home would you like to be?* If your response is, "I'd like to stay at home" your college options obviously are going to be constrained by geography, which is perfectly fine if that is what you want and need. As a commuter, you will need to work out the logistics of getting to and from college. This will probably involve your parents or guardians until you are of age to drive yourself. Public transportation may also be an option, depending on where you reside. If you plan to leave your hometown for college, it will be helpful for you to consider how often you expect to visit your family and friends. Making a trip home on an occasional weekend may be more feasible in terms of time and cost if you attend a college nearby or at least in the same region of the U.S. Others may be perfectly content attending a school across the U.S. or perhaps even abroad. My own research (Muratori, 2003; Muratori, Colangelo, & Assouline, 2003) has led me to believe that it is not necessarily the *actual* distance from home that matters as much as the *perceived* distance from home. A student who is 2 hours from home might experience more homesickness than one who moved across the nation to attend college. So, ask yourself, "How far is too far and how close is too close?" Regardless of your perception, choosing a college that is relatively close to home makes a lot of sense if you enter college at a particularly young age, because it will make it much easier for you to be involved in family events. Surely your parents (who may be responsible for your transportation for some time to come) will agree that the closer the proximity your school is to home, the more convenient it will be for them.

2 *How important is geographical location in your college selection?* A related question to the one above is whether there are certain regions of the U.S. to which you are most drawn. Factors other than how close or far away you want to be from home may affect your preferences. For instance, think about climate. Are there certain weather conditions that you would like to experience or avoid? (Prior to leaving Southern California, I admittedly thought questions about weather were superficial and irrelevant because there are no real weather changes in Southern California; however, after moving to the Midwest and then to the East Coast, I experienced "weather" for the first time and now understand how difficult it can be to adjust to different climates). You must remember that you are going to spend the next few years in college, so factors such as weather really can matter. For instance, some areas tend to get a lot of rain and/or may be cloudy and gray much of the time. This type of weather makes some people feel depressed, so spending several years in that environment would not be pleasant for them or even good for their health. In addition, are you more comfortable in an urban, rural, or suburban setting? What type of geographical environments will afford you the opportunity to do recreational and leisure activities that you enjoy? It is important to think beyond academics. This ties in to the next question.

3 *What are your extracurricular interests and which colleges have the resources to enable you to pursue your nonacademic interests?* One of the advantages of technology is that a person can easily obtain a wealth of information about virtually anything via the Internet. So, as you are gathering information about academic programs and financial aid on university Web sites, you should take the extra few moments to investigate university-sponsored social and extracurricular offerings and get information about the surrounding community. One caveat is that if you do enter college early, you will most likely be at a disadvantage to play intercollegiate sports wherever you attend college. Intramural sports are often available to early entrants; however, if you are a serious athlete, you might choose to reassess your decision to enter college early. It will be important for you to reflect on your priorities and determine how much you want athletics to be a part of your life.

4 *What are your tentative plans for a college major and what type of college/university will help you to pursue your academic interests?* If you are not sure about your educational or career direction, it might be wise to consider schools that are strong in a variety of subject areas. You may prefer a program that will give you a solid liberal arts background, in which case you probably would eliminate colleges that focus exclusively on technology. On the other hand, if you feel passionate about pursuing a career in science, math, or technology, and know that you do not want to major in the humanities or arts, you might find your optimal fit at an institution emphasizing the sciences or technology. One consideration is that because you are younger than most college applicants, you may have less clarity about your direction because you have had less time to develop your interests. You may be aware that it is common for traditional freshmen to change their majors several times—so don't worry if you haven't figured it all out yet! Understandably, as a young college entrant, you may feel even more uncertain than your older counterparts—and that is to be expected. With that said, you may have regrets later on if you prematurely foreclose on educational or career options. So, give yourself the space and time that you need to explore subject areas that may be of interest to you and choose colleges/universities that will afford you that flexibility.

5 *To what extent does the size of the institution matter to you? Would you prefer to attend a small, medium, or large school?* Although there is no right or wrong answer to these questions, you may discover that you have a stronger preference for one size or another. Quite literally, one size does not fit all! One can make general assumptions about campus life at institutions of various sizes (e.g.,

155

smaller campuses might offer more personalized attention and a sense of community, whereas larger universities may lack these attributes yet make up for them by offering students a much wider array of course options). In some cases, these assumptions may be correct; however, there may be exceptions. Some larger universities have established learning communities in residence halls and other programs to help students feel connected to each other, as well as to the institution. Both large and small colleges/universities want to help their students make a smooth adjustment to college and help them find their niche on campus. In a sense, they are attempting to give students the best of both worlds. Some smaller colleges have made arrangements with other schools to allow their students to take classes at other colleges, which greatly increases their course options and resources. For instance, there is a cluster of fine colleges in the northeastern region of the U.S. that have a reciprocity agreement with one another:

> Through the Five College Consortium—Mount Holyoke, Amherst, Hampshire, and Smith Colleges, and the University of Massachusetts at Amherst—you can enjoy the vast resources of not just one but four prominent colleges and a flagship research university at no additional cost. A free bus connects the Five Colleges, which are within a 12-mile radius. (Mount Holyoke College, n.d., ¶ 1)

On the West Coast, a similar arrangement has been established between Claremont McKenna College, Harvey Mudd College, Pitzer College, Pomona College, Scripps College, and two graduate colleges:

> The Claremont Colleges is a consortium of five undergraduate colleges and two graduate institutions and a central organization that provides services shared by all students, faculty, and staff. The eight institutions support and strengthen each other to become more than the sum of their parts, and

all but one are located on adjacent campuses. The Colleges are nationally and internationally renowned for academic excellence. Students at The Claremont Colleges enjoy the individualized academic attention of a small college and the resources of a major university. The Colleges not only share a library system, athletic facilities, and extra-curricular activities, but also offer joint academic programs and cross-registration in courses. Currently the consortium has over 6,000 students and a combined faculty and staff of over 3,300 members. More than 2,500 courses are available to students in Claremont. (Claremont Colleges, n.d., ¶ 1).

6 *To what extent is cost an issue? How much can your family afford to invest in your undergraduate education?* An important part of your search for a college is to investigate how much it will cost for you to attend colleges that are of interest to you. This information should be readily available on college Web sites. If you are considering private colleges or universities, the price tag of a 4-year education may be rather steep. The same may hold true if you are interested in a public university outside of your home state; however, you must remember that financial aid and scholarships are usually available.

Without question, need-based aid is far more plentiful than merit-based awards. Many families who are neither poor enough to qualify for financial aid nor rich enough to be comfortable paying full price understandably feel enormous pressure to somehow make ends meet to send their children away to college. Although it may require more effort on your and your parents' parts to apply for merit-based scholarships, which may be offered directly through colleges/universities, as well as outside sources, this is an option worth pursuing. In the appendix, I have included a list of financial aid resources that will provide you with more information about options and opportunities.

Narrowing Down Options

Narrowing down your list of prospective colleges may leave you feeling as if you are lost in a maze. Answering the questions posed in this chapter may help to give this process some direction so that you can avoid feeling overwhelmed. As the following parent and student perspectives illustrate, an important step is to identify your needs, as well as the factors that should be weighed most heavily in your decision.

Because of my daughter's AP scores, we let her know that college could be an option for her. We visited a few universities in the Midwest and South and at each place, she met with the director of admissions. At one university, although we didn't have an appointment, and a young woman in admissions first said that all students had to have high school diplomas, the number "34" (her ACT score) was magical. We all determined that a university in the South seemed to fit her needs the best, in large part because of high-quality academics *and* proximity to her family—since she couldn't drive. (Parent perspective)

By far the biggest factor was location; the university I attend is just a few blocks away from my house. While in high school, it was convenient to take classes there, so when I entered full-time I was already fairly familiar with the school. Also, [although] there are some other colleges nearby, the one I attend is by far the highest quality of them. (Student perspective)

Our primary concern was the social fit. We knew our son was academically ready, and probably had been for some time. We also were concerned whether the college was good enough. Because of his age, he needed to attend college locally and live at home, so his college choices were limited. We also were (and are) concerned about the consequent acceleration into grad school. We also had some concerns about whether he would be admitted and whether he would qualify for various scholarships. He proved to be competitive both for admission and for money. (Parent perspective)

We were aware of the early entrance programs. At the age at which these would have been academically appropriate for our child (age 10–14?), he was too young and not socially mature enough to live away from home. Also, it seemed unlikely to us that the early entry programs would be able to handle his lopsided academics (prior to his full-time college enrollment, he was supplementing his high school curriculum with 400- and sometimes 500-level math and computer science classes). We also had concerns about the quality of the academic programs at many of these, particularly the one in our home state, which is relatively new and located at a university [that] is not generally thought to be comparable to two or three of the universities located in our metro area. (Parent perspective)

By the time I was ready to make my choice about colleges, I had narrowed down my list to four schools. With four other siblings, my parents would not be able to pay for my entire college education without considerable financial aid, so finances played an important role in my decision. I also decided that I would like, if possible, to attend a school with an accessible hospital (whether or not it was directly associated with the school), as I am considering medical school and would like to be able to make an educated decision on my career path. I want to be able to volunteer and/or observe physicians on a regular basis. I also wanted to attend a school with [a] strong engineering [program], as this is probably the field I will study. (Student perspective)

The university I chose is one of Australia's leading universities for external students. Australia is a very urbanized country and most people go to a university in their home city; my university is in a small town, so it actually has more off-campus students than on-campus students! It has a reasonably good academic standing overall and was flexible to consider alternate high school qualifications (as I had an American high school diploma). (Student perspective)

Conclusion

Students of high ability who love learning and are eager to be in a challenging academic environment may find the college selection process to be overwhelming at first; however, approaching college selection in a systematic way, by answering the questions presented in this chapter, may alleviate some of the pressure. Adding colleges or universities to one's list and eliminating other schools from consideration by assessing their fit is an important step in the process. This may be easier said than done, especially if a student's goals are out of focus or if he or she has not engaged in self-exploration to identify his or her needs or differentiated his or her own needs, wishes, and goals from his or her parents' needs, wishes, and goals. Chapter 8 is written with the assumption that the college selection process has already occurred, so before proceeding forward, it is useful to reflect on the questions presented in this chapter.

What to Do Before You Leave for College

Focus Questions for Students

- Do you identify yourself as a procrastinator? If so, which of the items on your "to do" list are you most inclined to put off until the last minute or not do at all?

- You will notice that my "don't" list for you is rather short. What suggestions have others made to you regarding what you should and should not do as you prepare for college?

- Have a conversation with people you know who have gone away to college (parents, older siblings and friends, mentors, and the like). What did they find most helpful in their preparation for college? If they are willing to disclose this information, ask them to share their "don'ts" with you.

Introduction

Let's fast forward. I want you to imagine that you have narrowed down your options and after thoughtful consideration and many discussions with your parents, you have applied to several colleges that would make a fine choice. In fact, we will fast forward even further to the time after you have received the fantastic news that you have been accepted to College/University X.

(By the way, congratulations!) Perhaps you have even committed to one choice. (Yes, I know I have leaped over some pretty important steps—essentially the entire application and acceptance process—but because there are many excellent books available on the topic [see appendix], I figured you wouldn't mind if I left out that information.)

While we are still imagining the future, I want you to envision the period of time between sending in your acceptance form and packing your belongings to head off to college. Are you there with me? Assuming you are, I want you to consider what feelings and thoughts you might experience. Excitement and happiness because you were accepted to a great college? Nervousness because you don't exactly know what to expect and because you don't know how your age will impact your college experience? Eagerness to start a new chapter in your life? Relief that the application and selection process is over—finally? Perhaps a combination of all of the above and many other thoughts and feelings would be my guess. While you are still projecting into the future, I want to discuss a few things that you can do before you leave for college that will help to make your college adjustment smoother. In my view, these suggestions are applicable not only to students entering college early, but also to students entering college on a more traditional timeline.

Creating Your to Do List

Writing a list of actions you can take now to prepare yourself for college may help you to feel empowered. I will offer a few suggestions that you can add to your to do list if they seem applicable to you (some students already do the following things), but the idea is for you to personalize your list and make it your own.

1 Take care of unfinished business at home before you leave. If you have unresolved problems with family members or friends, leaving for college without addressing the issues may be tempting, but ultimately not helpful. In my research, I found that students who were carrying on long-distance relationships with boyfriends or girlfriends back home had more tension in their everyday lives. When they experienced friction or conflict in these relationships, these students were not able to function well emotionally and socially, which sometimes negatively affected their academic performance and ability to feel connected to the university (Muratori, 2003).

2 Discuss and negotiate with your parents how you might handle different expectations and rules when you visit home and when you are away at college. Although supervised by a resident advisor, students who live in residence halls function independently for the most part. You must make your own decisions about balancing study time with social activities, how late you will stay up at night, what you will eat and wear, and more. With a newfound sense of control over how you spend your time, you might feel confused about different role expectations when you come home for occasional weekends or vacations and discover different rules. It will be entirely up to you and your parents to reevaluate expectations and degrees of freedom (and if you have a background in statistics, I don't mean that in the statistical sense).

3 If you know that you have or suspect that you have medical problems, learning disabilities, other disabilities, or emotional/mental health issues that could potentially be problematic when you are in college, seek the professional help that you need in order to get the issues under control before you leave. Also, collaborate with your parents and/or helping professionals to develop a plan for how you will manage your problem or issue when you are on your own. Look into the university's counseling or health center for services you can take advantage of once you are on campus.

163

4 If you haven't already done so, start to address any deficits that you have in terms of study skills, habits, and time management. As is true for many of the students who responded to my questionnaire, these skills don't automatically appear once a student starts college—even if the student is brilliant. So, even though you do not have a lot of time before you start college, read up on ways to improve these skills and start practicing them as soon as possible. (See appendix for resources on these topics.) If you put your mind to it, you can alter poor work habits.

5 If you have a major gap in knowledge because you have not been exposed to a particular subject area and if you think this may become an obstacle for you, you could spend some time over the summer filling in the gaps on your own or taking a distance education course or intensive summer program in the subject.

6 Reflect on assumptions and expectations you have about college academically, socially, and emotionally. Distinguish between realistic and unrealistic expectations. In my counseling and research experience, I discovered that some early entrants held unrealistically high expectations about what their college experiences were going to be like, which ultimately resulted in disappointment (Muratori, 2003). On the other hand, some of the early entrants had college experiences that exceeded their expectations, which was very exciting for them. Early in the process, when you are visiting colleges, arrange to talk to college students to get their candid views about their experiences. This may help you to assess whether or not your expectations are reasonable. Although it is impossible for you to know with 100% certainty what lies ahead and how you will react to a situation, it will be helpful to at least think about and clarify your assumptions and expectations in advance so you will feel more prepared to handle potentially difficult situations.

7 Although an entire chapter was devoted to the topic of success, I will briefly offer the suggestion here to reflect on your short- and long-term goals (to the extent that you have formed them) and what it means in your eyes to be successful. You may change your goals as you are introduced to new ideas and subjects, but it will help you to stay focused (an attribute that consistently is mentioned among students who thrive in college) if you enter college with clear goals, at least for the short term.

8 Be prepared to take charge of your college experience. Rather than take a passive stance and wait for your needs to be met (whatever they may be) by someone else, take initiative to fulfill your own needs (only when it is within your power, of course). Without being aggressive or overbearing, you can assertively ask for what you need. If you need help from a professor or a teaching assistant (TA), visit him or her during office hours sooner rather than later. If you find a particular professor or instructor to be less than inspiring (to say it nicely), rather than mentally "check out" in class and allow your grade to slip because of the poor instruction, vow to take responsibility for your academic performance. Find other ways to learn the material if need be. Hopefully you will have excellent instructors (and often this will be the case), but regardless of where you attend college, you may encounter one or two professors with an undesirable teaching style, annoying habits, or unreasonable expectations. Despite this, the course grade will appear on your academic record— not the instructor's. Taking responsibility for one's actions is not always fun and life is not always fair. (The instructor of my undergraduate biology course who was long overdue for retirement once failed a student for missing an exam. The student missed it because she was in the hospital giving birth to her child. He accepted no excuses!) Nevertheless, taking charge of your life is a necessary part of growing up and actually feels empowering once you get the hang of it.

9 Although many of the items on your to do list involve preparing yourself mentally and psychologically for the college experience, you also need to attend to the practical aspects of getting ready. What belongings are you going to bring with you and what are you going to leave at home with your parents? It will be helpful for you to have a conversation with your future roommate during the summer to discuss large items that you plan to bring. This will help you to avoid duplication of certain items such as your television or microwave (that is, if they are permitted in your dorm

165

room) that can be shared. You may also need to go shopping for clothes (personally, I love this part of preparation. I'll use any excuse!), school supplies, and books. Once you have registered for fall classes, you may have access to information about the required and recommended textbooks for your courses. Some students wait until the semester begins to purchase books (new and/or used) at the college bookstore; however, you can expect large crowds and must prepare to wait in long lines. An alternative is to order the books online (and if you get lucky, sometimes at a discounted price).

10 If you haven't had a conversation with your parents about budgeting your money, now would be a good time. Discuss with them what your spending limits will be before heading off to college so that you will be clear about their expectations. Learn the financial basics—how to create a budget, how to balance a checkbook, how to track your accounts online, and how to avoid credit card debt. Trust me—your parents will be thrilled to have this conversation with you.

11 If you have never done a load of laundry, you are going to need to learn. Part of gaining independence involves laundry—and lots of it! Learn how to separate whites from brights (unless you want your white underwear to turn pink), remember that cotton shrinks, and that Tide is the best (just kidding—kind of). Remember that your sheets should be changed more than once a semester and above all, start saving your coins now.

12 Most important of all, take your to do list and actually do the things on your list.

Creating Your Don't List

One way to approach this list is to take your to do list and write down the opposite of each suggestion; however, I would like to add a couple of don'ts to the list:

1 Don't slack off at your current school and think that your last semester grades don't count because you already have been accepted to college. Colleges and universities can always change their mind if a student's grades take a nosedive, so to speak.

2 Don't wait until the last minute to get started on your to do list. If you are a procrastinator, your tendency might be to wait until a few days before you leave home to tie up loose ends. My advice to you—just don't!

Conclusion

This chapter admittedly was brief in comparison to other chapters of this book; however, my brevity in no way reflects the relative importance of the ideas expressed. Sending in your acceptance letter and acknowledging your commitment to attend a particular institution may feel like a weight has been lifted. That is to be expected because the act of making an important decision and closing doors to other options (at least for now) is a major step forward. Be sure to celebrate—you deserve it! At the same time, you must also prepare for the major life transition that you are about to experience. College can be one of the most memorable and exciting experiences of your life, so taking a proactive stance and tackling the to do's on your list *before* you start college will help to make your adjustment smoother once you arrive on campus. More helpful tips will be presented in Chapter 9, when the discussion shifts to what you can do to help yourself succeed after you are a full-fledged college student.

167

The College Experience: Getting Off to a Strong Start and Maintaining Momentum

Focus Questions for Students:

- In your own estimation, how well have you handled transitions in your life? How adaptable have you been to new experiences and changes? As past behavior is thought to be the best predictor for future behavior, how do you think you will adapt to college?

- How do you react when you experience a minor setback (e.g., a lower grade than you expected, not being the top student in class)? Ask your parents for feedback regarding their perceptions of how you handle setbacks.

- If you intend to be a residential college student, what aspects of the dorm experience are you looking forward to? What aspects, if any, do you have concerns about?

- Is there anything that would lead you to make a u-turn and return to high school if college proves to be considerably more challenging (academically, socially, or emotionally) than you expect? If you discover after entering college that you took the wrong path, what alternative path would you pursue?

Making a Positive Adjustment to College

As much as I would like to, I cannot offer you step-by-step instructions for making an easy adjustment to college or university life. Due to individual differences, I suspect that the steps one must take need to be modified for each person in accordance with his or her strengths and relative weaknesses; however, I can offer general suggestions that may promote a positive adjustment for both residential and commuter students.

Develop a Reasonable Program of Study

Give yourself a fair chance to succeed and get off to a strong start by working with your academic advisor to develop a schedule that works for you. Know your personal limits and be careful not to be overly ambitious when putting together your first semester's course schedule. Account for the fact that some of your energy may be invested in adjusting to various aspects of college. You will learn a great deal about how to navigate through college after you have completed a semester. You will have a much better idea about what courses tend to be like in terms of rigor and homework, so it will be easier to determine how heavy a course load you can comfortably manage in future semesters.

Exercise Good Study Habits, Time Management Skills, and Self-Discipline on a Consistent Basis

As I mentioned previously, strong work habits tend not to appear overnight. You should try to develop these skills before you enter college full time so that when you start, you can hit the ground running. The critical word here is *consistency*. If you are well-prepared for some exams, but not for others, your course grade will suffer: " . . . because college midterms and final examinations tend to carry more weight in determining one's grade [than middle school or high school exams], it is especially important to be vigilant about keeping up with readings and assignments" (Muratori, 2006, p. 31).

Set Goals and Develop a Concrete Plan to Accomplish Them

If you are academically driven, you may think that goals are primarily related to academics and careers. Although these types of goals are very important, so are goals related to your social and personal life. As a college student, you will have an exponentially greater number of academic, social, and extracurricular opportunities than you have had in the past. Discover the ways in which these opportunities can assist you in developing and reaching your goals. For instance, whether your desire is to become a more effective public speaker, become more open-minded, or develop a particular skill, you may be able to find a club or organization on campus that will help you work toward your goal. As you develop intellectually, personally, and socially, your goals may change. One suggestion is to articulate your goals and the steps you will take to achieve them in specific terms. For instance, rather than saying " I want to broaden my view on culture," you might say, " I will broaden my view of culture X by attending two meetings per month of the culture X club and attending two cultural events this semester sponsored by the club." It is much easier to measure goals when you know exactly what you are measuring.

Use Community and Campus Resources

In both my clinical and research roles, I observed a striking difference between the adjustment of early entrants who made use of the resources that were offered to them and the adjustment of those who did not use them. High-ability students who are accustomed to doing things on their own and figuring out their own problems may find it difficult to admit to needing a tutor or a counselor when they enter college. Although I certainly appreciate the struggle, I also know that students can reduce, if not prevent, the effect of problems spiraling out of control by seeking assistance when they need it (and not waiting too long). Using available resources is essential to taking charge of your college experience.

Deal Effectively With Multipotentiality—Having Too Many Choices

If your talents and interests span several areas, you may have what educators and researchers refer to as *multipotentiality*. It's wonderful to have multiple talents, but it can also be stressful when eventually you are forced to prioritize them. Students who are fearful of deciding on a college major or career path may make a hasty decision to get the ordeal over with as soon as possible. The wrong decision, however, may lead to feelings of regret. So, why hurry? As a young entrant, you should be *exploring* your options, not narrowing them prematurely at this point in your life. Narrowing will come gradually as you discover your true passions and learn about the world of work. As you engage in the process, you may be introduced to new subject areas that you love, or you may discover career fields that will allow you to combine several interests. You may decide to select one focus for your career and relegate other interests to be avocations that you pursue in your free time. Giving yourself permission to not have all of the answers about your future direction and career when you start college hopefully will help to reduce your stress to some degree.

Find Balance

I must confess that I have not mastered this task; however, it definitely seems worthy of striving toward. Finding balance in life as a college student may seem an impossible feat, but my point in adding it to this list is to emphasize that your college experience should be much more than jumping through a bunch of academic hoops. If you are hoping to have a meaningful college experience, you should be mindful of what is important to you. Define for yourself what optimal balance in your life would look like. For some, it may involve devoting equal time to coursework and extracurricular activities. Others may try to find balance by taking elective courses that require them to use different skill sets than they ordinarily use (e.g., a biochemistry major may take art classes). Again, it is up to you to determine what will constitute a meaningful and balanced college experience.

Make Connections on Campus

Researchers who study college adjustment have pointed out how important it is for students to feel that they matter. Schlossberg, Lynch, and Chickering (1989) suggested that students who feel noticed, depended upon, and appreciated by their universities will feel more invested in higher education. This makes intuitive sense. One of the reasons that residence hall communities are thought to be such an integral part of the college experience is that they promote this sense of "mattering." According to Gerdes and Mallinckrodt (1994):

> important elements of social adjustment include becoming integrated into the social life of college, forming a support network, and managing new social freedoms. Some of the most commonly reported crises in the freshmen year involve difficulties in social adjustment manifested as feelings of homesickness and loneliness. Social support networks are an extremely important component of college adjustment, and perceptions of insufficient social support have been shown to predict attrition for both Black students and White students. (p. 281)

There are many pathways to finding a sense of connection on campus. Even if you decide to commute to college and live

173

at home with your parents, you can still take the initiative to develop connections with teachers, mentors, and networks of friends or peers, which may help you to feel attached to the college or university that you are attending.

Moving Into the Residence Hall

Imagine that the big day has arrived. With the help of your parents, you move your belongings into your new home—the residence hall. You see a lot of new faces and wonder how you will fit in and who will become your friends. Many questions cross your mind, and you can be certain that the other students are asking themselves the same questions. At some point in the day, you and your parents exchange hugs and goodbyes and they wish you well before getting in the car to head back home.

As you eagerly and perhaps nervously anticipate your new life as a full-time college student, your feelings about ending the previous chapter in your life may surface. That is to be expected. Like many other college students (not just early entrants), you may experience a touch of homesickness and sadness about parting with your family and friends at home. It would not be surprising if these feelings emerged several weeks earlier, as you were preparing to leave. Transitions in life tend to be stressful, and moving away from home and into a residence hall often requires a major adjustment not only for students, but also for parents. The following tips are intended to help you successfully navigate your way through the residential portion of your college experience.

Deal Effectively With Social Distractions in the Residence Hall

174

Effectively dealing with social distractions does not mean that one should either avoid social situations altogether or regularly succumb to distractions. Even if you reside in an honors dorm, you can expect to encounter distractions of many types. Loud music, chatty roommates, impromptu and planned parties down the hall, and invitations to hang out in a friend's room and carry on philosophical debates late into the night are a few examples of the types of distractions you may experience. Then, of course, there are the temptations of video games and the Internet. Some students may have no trouble setting appropriate boundaries with others (and themselves), maintaining their focus on academics, and allowing themselves to indulge in social activities only when they truly have the time. Other students who are inclined to procrastinate may welcome the excuse—any excuse—to not study and may have more difficulty learning to stay on top of academics while enjoying the social aspects of being part of the college community. Students who join sororities and fraternities also face this challenge. Strategies that may be helpful include scheduling study time in quiet places (e.g., the library) on a regular basis, getting in the routine of working on assignments in between classes or at certain times, and incorporating more structure into one's schedule. In college there is a lot more time spent outside the classroom than inside; thus, students must take responsibility for structuring their time wisely.

Communicate Effectively and Negotiate Conflicts With Roommates

Just because two students share commonalities such as high ability and status as early entrants (if they are attending a special program), it does not mean that they will be compatible as roommates. Like any two strangers who are paired to live together, early entrants sharing a dorm room are expected to coexist somewhat peacefully in a relatively small space with little privacy. That would be a challenge for even the most accommodating individuals. When individuals with differing lifestyles, personalities, temperaments, and notions of cleanliness/neatness are assigned to room with each other, conflicts may erupt at some point in time. For some, the potential for conflict becomes evident the first time

175

they meet. For others, it may take some time before tension surfaces. There may even be some who are fortunate enough to get along splendidly with their roommates. One of the challenges that comes with this type of living arrangement is the opportunity for roommates to negotiate conflicts with each other and learn how to communicate more effectively. An early entrant who resides with an older student may face these challenges, as well as a different type of challenge; due to their difference in age, the older roommate may engage in social experiences from which the early entrant is excluded.

Address Personal Issues

Personal issues such as depression, alcohol abuse, family issues, and homesickness need to be addressed. Adjusting to college can be a stressful period in a student's life regardless of when he or she starts college, and it tends to be especially difficult for individuals who are battling a serious issue such as depression, alcohol abuse, and/or family conflict. Although it is best if these problems are addressed before a student leaves for college, realistically, they sometimes surface or are exacerbated after he or she arrives on campus and is away from home. For some individuals who have been diagnosed with clinical depression or have a chronic issue, I suspect that waiting an extra year or so before starting college would not necessarily lead to a different outcome. If the condition is thought to be worsened due to a student's lack of maturity, perhaps college entrance should be delayed by a year or two. On the other hand, if the condition will persist regardless of timing and if the student is ready for college in all other respects, delaying college entrance might not be the best option. In any case, a student dealing with such a condition needs to identify and use the appropriate resources and services available on campus or through the early entrance program.

Sometimes students are caught off guard by intense feelings of homesickness that they never expected to feel. Homesickness may be manifested in a number of ways including somatic symptoms, eating or sleeping irregularities, intense sadness, or as one early entrant put it, a persistent "dull ache." In some cases, these feelings may prevent students from establishing connections on campus, which may lead to isolation. One student who experienced severe homesickness and was later diagnosed with clinical depression found it nearly impossible to feel connected and involved in campus life. As an observer pointed out, " her real issue was that 90% of her was back home." Students may be reluctant to seek support when homesickness strikes; however, there really is no need for them to suffer in silence. Homesickness is an issue that student development experts, residence hall staff, and college counselors are well trained to deal with.

Exercise Good Judgment Regarding Underage Drinking, Drugs, and Sexual Activity

One of the reasons that admissions directors and early entrance program administrators place a tremendous amount of weight on applicants' maturity is that they want to be confident that their students have the capacity to exercise good judgment. Although no student is expected to be perfect, one who lacks the maturity to make healthy decisions about behaviors that could have serious consequences is a student who is not ready to be living away from home and in college. Students must have the maturity to function independently and make good decisions on a daily basis. Lapses in judgment about relatively benign matters (e.g., staying up too late one night chatting with your roommate) may have minor consequences; however, in extreme instances, lapses of judgment regarding potentially dangerous behaviors may result in expulsion, suspension, alcohol or drug addiction, pregnancy, or even death.

Making a U-Turn: Considerations When Early Entrance Proves Not to Be the Optimal Path

Two concepts that have been threads throughout this book are decision making and informed risk-taking. Hopefully, I have made it abundantly clear that choosing a particular path, whether it is early college entrance, entry after senior year, or even re-entry into college at some point down the road, involves not one decision or risk, but multiple decisions and multiple risks. Life involves risks, and even though we may do our best to select options that minimize potential risks, we cannot eliminate them altogether. Most students who choose early entrance after thoughtful consideration of feasible options do extremely well in college academically, socially, and emotionally (Brody, Muratori, & Stanley, 2004). However, a few won't succeed.

Perhaps it is my own defense mechanism, but when I have to take a risk, it helps me to consider in advance how I might handle the worst-case scenario. By recognizing that at worst, it will not destroy me, I find it easier to muster up the courage to take the risk. So, I encourage you to try this strategy. What would you do if you (as the student or parent) realize that the particular path you (or your child) pursued did not work out? Consider the following options:

- return to high school and graduate with high school classmates,
- leave the university or college and be homeschooled prior to reentering college elsewhere at a later time,
- transfer to a different college or university that is a better fit, or
- pursue a nonacademic path for a period of time before reentering college.

As you can see, several options exist. By establishing a backup plan, you may feel more confident to handle any dreaded situation should it arise.

Because research on the experiences of early entrants who have returned to high school is very limited, I am not qualified to suggest that going back to high school is either a wise or unwise choice. Again, I suspect that each individual case is different and involves unique circumstances that should be taken into account. To illustrate this, I will share the case of a young woman who knew within the first week of college that she desperately wanted to go home; however, she suffered through one semester largely because she was concerned about being judged negatively by people back home for quitting. Unfortunately, when she did return to high school, despite support from her friends, certain high school faculty members were not as sensitive. As her mother recalled,

> One of the teachers even made the remark . . . that they didn't know why she came back or why she couldn't make it work there. . . . I think it was the principal who said that, so she kind of felt hurt by that. And maybe she felt she didn't fit in anywhere.

Although this student initially was happy to be back at home, she soon discovered that "once you leave, it's almost impossible to go back, and if you do, it's not going to be a good time. It's kind of a final decision you make." Having had a taste of college, she was ready to move forward with her life, not backward, and she discovered that the problems that made her want to leave high school in the first place (e.g., the immaturity of her peers) were still there. This student admittedly regretted her decision to return to high school and wished that others had not made it as easy for her to return: "If I had stayed one more semester, I probably would have been a lot happier there. I think I got the idea in my head that I could go back and so then it made it more difficult to be there." On a positive note, she reentered college a semester later at a university that was more suitable for her in terms of its proximity to her home and the diversity of the student body. She claimed to be very happy.

One lesson to learn from this student's experience is that those who are dissatisfied with their college experience should not be too hasty to abandon their college plans and return home prematurely. Their discomfort may be temporary. Nevertheless, when the student-environment match clearly proves to be poor for any number of reasons, making a u-turn and returning to high school is only one option. Although some students may be comfortable with the idea of returning to the high school environment that they left, others might choose a different direction; perhaps make a right turn or a left turn instead of a u-turn. Making the wrong decision about early college entrance does not have to result in going down a dead end road and being stuck. Being cognizant that still one has options even when the original plan does not work out is very important.

Students' Comments About Their College Experiences

Student contributors were asked to share both the positive and negative experiences they had in college. These students describe their various opportunities and challenges. Reading the following excerpts might help you consider what you can do to prepare yourself for your college experience.

It was a successful year. I changed majors a couple of times, going from political science to classics, and then adding an international relations major. Despite tackling a difficult and full course load, I managed to get out of it with a 3.9 GPA. I loved the honors courses. They've been, hands down, the most interesting courses I've taken in college. Besides that, I've worked as a producer over at the university's television station. I produced a live debate show once a week. I joined the Student Speaker's Bureau, a group formed to encourage the development of public speaking skills at the university (which has very few courses on the subject). I entered a speech competition, and placed second, winning $150. I regularly went to my professors' office hours, forming a few close relationships. I'm even working as a research assistant next semester for one of my international relations professors. I presented at a research conference. I [have] hosted prospective early entrants, giving them a taste of campus life. On the weekends I [go] out with my friends ... I even managed to convince my girlfriend to go on a trip with me, which resulted in us getting lost. I like to think of it as a learning experience. I remember being disappointed about receiving my first A-. Ancient Greek had managed to get the best of me. At that point I realized that I might not be able to coast through college as easily as I did high school, but I wouldn't have it any other way. (Entered program at age 17.)

I loved how easy it was to adjust for me; I never thought of or introduced myself as an early entrant, I was just a college freshman. I met amazing people, improved myself as a writer and student, and I joined an a cappella singing group. College so far is the best, most challenging time of my life! (Entered program at age 17.)

It was a lot of work, but overall I enjoyed it. Going in I did not think I would have to do so many all-nighters as I did! (Entered college at age 17)

Well, first semester—actually the first two—didn't go as well as I'd hoped, but I'm bringing my grades back up. Joining the [marching band] was probably one of my better decisions; it's a lot of fun. I also joined Phi Mu Alpha. I never would have thought I would join a fraternity, but it has been pretty fun and, generally, a good experience. (Entered college at age 17.)

Leaving New York was fairly miserable and the program both provided little to no support for student extracurricular life while repressing strongly drug and alcohol use and thus parties, driving them underground and making them small and somewhat sketchy. In short: the social scene was not my scene. But I had one amazing professor and a number of really good ones and I made some pretty good friends and discovered some excellent films and music. All in all, I think I would have probably preferred to have spent another year at Stuyvesant and then had the full 4 years at the university where I am currently enrolled and am very happy. Transferring is an awkward experience socially—although I am currently pretty happy with my friends—and deprives you of a lot of the experience of going to a college together with folks, growing with them, failing and succeeding with them, etc. Also it tends to impede the process for things like getting recs [recommendations] for fellowships when there are no professors you've known for more than a year. (Entered program at age 16.)

My experience at college is somewhat abnormal. I currently play on two U.S. athletic teams. My life revolves between the two poles of athletics and academics, with relatively little in between. During the week, I work out at the athletic center and do my schoolwork. On weekends I am invariably training. When my parents were still curious enough to ask me what my life was like at college, I would generally say that my life consisted of my room, the dining hall, the classrooms, and the weight room. This is more or less true, and I have led a somewhat sequestered life for the past 2 years. This self-imposed semimonasticism is controlled by two factors—the heavy academic and athletic workload I have, as well as the fact that I do not find the average early entrant at this school to be "my type of person." Although I have relatively good relations with many people, and a tight group of close friends, my personality and lifestyle is somewhat at odds with the rest of the college [students], who tend to lead more "alternative" lifestyles than the relatively Spartan one that I do. Although I occasionally feel somewhat alienated from my peers for personal reasons, as well as the fact that I am not around frequently, I feel comfortable and enjoy myself on campus. It is odd, however, to return home and spend time with the people I grew up with. Although my high school friends are still easygoing and welcoming, there is a tangible experience gap. I feel and act much older than they do, and adults tend to treat me as an adult. It can be a bit awkward talking with old friends, as one has a certain feeling of "talking down" to them, even if that is not the intention. But, it's still all good. (Entered program at age 16.)

My coursework (pre-med) was always difficult and required more studying than I was ever used to in high school, but it was manageable and interesting. I also joined the crew team, which took up many hours weekly and even daily, but it was a great experience and I plan to continue rowing next year. Living in a dorm was great, enabling me to meet and become close friends with many students and to have things to do at night. (Entered program at age 16.)

I love it. It's great! It's way challenging and wonderful! I don't like the rules or dorm director, but I've made wonderful friends! (Entered program at age 16.)

It has been a rough ride so far and it's far from over. However, every minute of it has been worthwhile for me. I've befriended some of the quirkiest professors that I'll probably ever meet and I've done some of the dumbest things I'll ever do. But, the best part about college is it's all OK!

I expected college to be different from high school, but not as radically as different as it felt to me. It all suddenly seemed so grown up. They aren't kidding when they say you won't be spoon fed. (Entered program at age 16.)

Academically, I am satisfied. I have an amazing relationship with my professors. They are so accessible and available, and are concerned not only with my academic progress, but also nonacademic pursuits. Personally, I feel like I got the independence that I longed for. I have been allowed to explore a variety of things in a liberal arts environment. Since I attend a small campus, I have been given opportunities to run things . . . and develop close relationships with my fellow students.

At the same time, I feel that socially it has been tough. A lot of people who are at the college are intelligent people who often lack social skills. They were awkward in [high school], hated it, and thought that early college was the way out. There are also those who were suffering from way too much teenage angst, and thought that leaving home would

183

help them resolve their anger. I hate this element of escapism because I don't view college as an escape. Having such a significant number of people who are in an escapist mode as my immediate source of social life, in an isolated campus, is not exactly the highlight of my college life.

Also, I feel that the school is so compelled to prove itself as on par with other colleges, that there's so much focus on academia. As students, we often lack balance, and are always buried in our schoolwork, that by the end of sophomore year, we're so burnt out. (Entered program at age 15.)

At college, I was able to take many more advanced classes than at high school. I've met many very close friends and learned to be a leader. The program has taught me a lot about living independently and in a community. (Entered program at age 15.)

Overall, I have enjoyed my time in college. [I was a commuter] and sometimes wished I had the chance to be a part of a school with more sense of community, and to live on campus altogether. For the first couple of years, I didn't really know what I wanted to do and I was dating a guy who wasn't right for me, but I eventually figured it all out. (Entered program at age 13.)

Conclusion

This chapter emphasized how crucial it is for college students to take charge of their experience. Residential college students experience a role shift once they enter college. Expected to accept responsibility for their behaviors, college students must be able to manage their time effectively, juggle many activities while designating enough time for studying, wake up on time, get to class on time, do homework assignments and turn them in on time without reminders from parents, negotiate conflicts with roommates, deal with distractions and set limits with others, do laundry and chores, budget their money, maintain a healthy lifestyle, and the list goes on. As a college student, it will be up to you to make good choices for your life. So, before turning the page to Chapter 10, ask yourself, "Am I ready for these challenges?"

10

Recommendations and Conclusion

Many different perspectives in addition to mine have been offered throughout this book. Given my belief that we can learn a great deal about a phenomenon from those who have experienced it first-hand, it wouldn't seem right to conclude this book by offering my recommendations only. I would like to share this last chapter with those who have so generously contributed their perspectives. Here are their pearls of wisdom.

Advice for Prospective Early Entrants From Early Entrants

Student contributors were asked to respond to the following question: What advice can you offer young entrants that will help them to be well-prepared for the academic, social, and emotional demands of college?

There's nothing you can prepare for, except the following: bring a good and humble attitude, don't be afraid to use your resources, be excellent, keep pursuing your dream no matter what, and most importantly, pace yourself. Don't

get too overwhelmed by lots of schoolwork and your social life. Try new things but don't let it consume you. (Entered program at age 17.)

Take as many AP classes as possible and enroll in part-time college courses [before you start full-time]. (Entered program at age 17.)

Keep focused and work hard. It goes by fast, so take the little time you have by the horns and do the best you can. (Entered program at age 17.)

Know what you are getting into, don't just know what you're getting away from. Make a conscious choice that you want to go to the early college [program] in question, not just that you want to leave your high school. I think issues at hand are more or less the same as those with any college, with the only real change being the age and maturity of the students. In my experience, early college students tend to be fairly intellectually mature but, if anything, this is negatively correlated with emotional maturity. (Entered program at age 16.)

Learn how to do laundry right before arriving; manage your money well (buying books, food, daily necessities, and sometimes fun stuff); resist going home every weekend if you happen to live nearby (you'll receive negative social feedback from dorm mates who either miss you or want to tease you); go to class! The notes they post online and that your friend took just aren't the same (also, do not miss labs); stay healthy (you can't study well or do anything well if you get sick); and make friends because college is so fun. (Entered program at age 16.)

Study, don't expect sleep, and have fun. Take time for yourself. (Entered program at age 16.)

It's one thing to master every course, but don't miss out on the moments you cherish and spend time with people you love. Moments are fleeting . . . but knowledge is forever. You will be learning new things for the rest of your life, so don't throw away the times that matter most. Also, don't get burned out! It's very tempting to go crazy with courses and workloads, but don't kill yourself. I'm sure you can handle that one extra class, but do you absolutely need to? I came to college thinking I would take 21 hours per semester for 2 years. Well, I did for two semesters and nearly fell apart. . . . I offer one piece of advice: It's simply not worth it. Don't throw away the most memorable time in your life—your youth—because it's never coming back. I learned this the hard way. (Entered program at age 16.)

Be willing to change and adapt. At college, you may realize that you have a love for a subject you once despised or that some people you might have hung out with before don't make good friends. You have to be willing to put forth the effort to change your study habits, your sleep schedule, and your time management skills in order to do well. (Entered program at age 16.)

Be focused on learning and not only on social things. Don't let your parents dominate your life or education (I've seen this a lot). Make friends and be nice to all your peers. Take advantage of your college's amenities (libraries, clubs, live music, and political events). Allow time for reflection on the process of growing up and being alive. (Entered program at age 16.)

Don't procrastinate. Keep your academic priorities in order at all times. Don't get behind in your work. It's difficult to catch up. Learn to study and manage your time. Shelve your pride and always ask for help if you need it. Most professors don't bite, and there are lots of tutoring services and study groups on campus. Make friends—they are good study buddies and are very supportive when you go through difficult circumstances . . . (Entered program at age 16.)

Practice self-discipline: Eat all your vegetables, exercise regularly, establish a routine for each day, plan ahead, take lots of notes, don't be intimidated by other people, choose friends wisely, do not cram, take interesting electives, don't be tempted to cheat, join a student organization, apply for scholarships/honors/awards, be a leader and role model, don't do anything illegal, develop good relationships with professors/school staff, take time to breathe, read a book, go for a walk, watch a movie, explore campus culture, learn an instrument and a language . . . find what you are good at . . . find out what you are bad at and make it better. Experience college to the lawful limits! (Entered program at age 15.)

The most important thing to keep in mind for young entrants is to be willing to ask for help. While most early college entrants are used to being the smartest in their class, college classes demand much more. Many might think of asking questions as a sign of weakness, but asking questions is a sign of strength. Have the courage to seek help and to actively engage in the learning process. . . . It's important to make friends and continue to keep in contact with old friends. I have found their support to be an important factor of success in college. (Entered program at age 15.)

Academic: Find something you love and get obsessed with it. Do the work because you love it . . . and do it even if no one is watching. Don't do well because you want to make the grade . . .

Social: Resign yourself. You're too young to have sex with, too young to go to the bars with, and too young to be even slightly cool. I don't believe it is possible to have a normal social life if you're entering college at an exceptionally young age. That said: keep your dorm room door open, go to all the campus activities, and volunteer to help with fun things. Being on the staff of a cool event will make you tons of friends. Oh, and at least during the last 2 years, not telling anyone my age really helped me out.

Emotional: Get obsessed with something—film, biology, guitar playing—just so long as there is one thing you can really devote yourself to. When I was having tough times, I'd ask myself, "Why am I even here?" and things were much easier once I could answer myself with, "To make movies, damn it!" (Entered college on her own at age 15.)

There is some amount of preparation that can be done, but mostly it depends on who you are naturally. You must already be motivated, smart, get along well with peers, and be strong in focus and character. Preparation might include academic things such as basic knowledge of math and English, but the rest must come from within. (Entered program at age 14.)

Well, I would say that if you are not driven and motivated, you might as well not consider early college. Other than that . . . get involved in peer groups early, try to have fun, and work [hard]. (Entered program at age 13.)

I guess I can really only offer advice about off-campus college study; I would say you need to be very personally motivated, able to cope with working alone, and prepared to sometimes feel isolated. I would imagine though that many people considering entering college early would have had this experience as homeschoolers.

With regards to on-campus study, like I said before, I felt that 13 was too young. I never completely fit in and shared the same experience or worldview. I had been at university lectures before and got this feeling. By 15, though, I no longer felt it would be a problem; now at 16 I would have no hesitation about going on campus with this 2-year age difference. More importantly I think I will get a lot more out of it—not just because I would fit in more easily, but because I can now really enjoy and be part of everything college life has to offer.

My other general advice would be not to be in any hurry to get into college. Without taking your eye off the goal, you should take your time and make sure you are as prepared as you can be, you understand how universities work, you know the terminology (undergraduate, postgraduate, . . . majors, etc.), and you're comfortable with reading and researching independently at a university level. Also, make sure you like your university, you've got into the best one you could, and you've chosen the right course [of study].

A big problem as an early entrant, particularly here in Australia where universities are very vocationally oriented, is the pressure to make a career decision at such a young age. This has been the hardest part for me, particularly as my preference is for the humanities rather than the sciences, and because I don't want to be an academic. The trick is to find a course [of study] that leaves your career choices open

191

while still being able to deliver job prospects, to get the best undergraduate degree you possible can, and to use your head start as a blessing instead of a disability. This is one of the main advantages of not rushing into college.

The other challenge of entering university, which I really enjoyed, was the adjustment to a new way of thinking and working. My distance high school experience was reading textbooks and answering multiple-choice questions; at university I had a small reading list, a choice of essay topics and an exam date half a year away! Luckily I had very good writing skills and within a few weeks I had adjusted to this new way of working and loved it. (Entered university at age 13 as a full-time distance student.)

Advice for Prospective Early Entrants From Resident Advisors

Resident advisors who supervise early entrance students were asked the following question: What advice do you have for prospective students who are considering applying to early entrance programs?

The advice that I would give for prospective students is know who you are and what you want out of the program before you get here. Accept now that you will change for the better or worst—that is up to you. There will be a lot of internal and external distractions that will be challenging, however, keep your eye on what you want out of the experience and be true to who you are. Get involved with your residence hall community and be a positive influence for others. Be willing to learn about people who are different than you are, they could become very good friends. Also, take advantage of the opportunities that are presented to you. The whole world can open up when you go to college; it is about making choices, make ones you will be proud of!

Early entrance to college is not for everyone, but it's definitely for more people than the general public thinks. With the proper support and structure, an early entrance program not only teaches students advanced academics, but it also teaches them something about life (getting to know others, struggling academically for the first time, and learning how to live outside the confines of home). I have met only a handful of students who have not enjoyed the experience. Even students who have done poor academically seem to truly enjoy the experience, despite their academic difficulty. Evaluate the program you are considering and consider best fit. The early entrance experience is what you make of it. A student who works hard, chats with professors, takes extra time on tests and assignments, and enjoys the academic playground of the college campus can do amazing things. That same student can also do the minimum, likely pass, but [his or her] journey may not be as fulfilling. The outcome lies in the hands of the student, once [he or she has] the minimum academic requirements.

Don't come to a program like this unless it is what you want (not your parents). Come for the right reasons. Have strong goals and a desire to succeed. Be aware of your own strengths and weaknesses. Be a leader, not a follower.

Come to college early for a reason and stay focused on that reason. Take a good look at why you want to go. It's easy to say that you want more than what your "stupid" high school can provide, but is it really what your high school lacks academically or are you more interested in getting out from under the teachers', administration's, and your parents' watchful eyes? Bernie Rodgers had a great way of putting it: the students hear "college" and all the freedoms they associate with it, and the parents hear "early" assuming that the college provides more structure than mainstream college. There is more support in many ways and more adult presence, but not more structure.

I don't think there are many students who can realistically assess what I have [addressed] above, so it is often a conversation with the parent who will have to take a real look at their child and either help [him or her] make a decision or make the decision for [him or her]. It can be hard for many parents who find it difficult to say "no" to their kid, but they must be realistic about what their child can handle and what [he or she] can't.

Advice for Prospective Early Entrants From Program Administrators

Program directors of selected early entrance programs were asked to respond to the following question: What advice do you have for prospective students who are considering applying to your program?

Take it seriously. Don't be afraid to ask for help. Get to know the adults around you—they are here to help. Be honest with everyone, including yourself. Study abroad. "Follow your bliss." Contribute. Believe me when I tell you college is different than high school and that your old habits will no longer work. Pick your friends carefully—choose people who will support your best interests instead of those who might bring you down. Get engaged in something on campus. Work hard, from the beginning. It's easier to scale back if you are overstudying than it is to catch up once you have dug a hole for yourself. Have fun.

—*Ms. Susan Colgate, Director of AAG*

Visit us. Visit other programs, as well. Many colleges are now offering students the opportunity of early entry. But, there are still just a handful of universities and colleges with the vision and resources to provide a supportive environment.

—Mr. Shailindar Singh, Interim Head of the Clarkson School

Please consider the normal path first and then get as much information as possible about the early entrance program of interest. For the right gifted student, an [early entrance program] can make a huge positive difference in their lives.

—Mr. Richard Maddox, Director of EEP at CSULA

Practice self-reliance at the academic and social level. Many [students] are ready academically but can't handle the social freedom.

—Ms. Lisa Whitaker, Director of GAMES

If you are ready, NAASE is a great program for you and your family.

—Dr. Nicholas Colangelo,
Director of the Belin-Blank Center and NAASE

Concentrate on the many opportunities. Don't dwell on what was left behind.

—Dr. Susan Assouline,
Associate Director of the Belin-Blank Center and NAASE

Seek a variety of challenges as often as possible and do not be afraid to take risks that promote growth. In the words of Helen Keller, "One should never consent to creep when one feels the impulse to soar."

—Dr. Elizabeth Connell, Director of PEG

195

Take the SAT and/or ACT early and often in order to maximize your opportunities for entry into the program. Also, make sure that you are prepared to leave everything that senior year of high school has to offer: friends, prom, senior events, AP and/or IB classes, "senioritis," etc.

We recommend that students visit USC to make sure that this is where they would like to attend college for the next 4 years. Students who apply to this program miss out on the opportunity to apply to a variety of colleges in their senior year. Our expectation is that students will complete their bachelor's degrees at USC.

—*Dr. Pennelope Von Helmolt, Director of RHP*

Students who are interested in applying to Simon's Rock College should visit our Web site and learn about the kinds of students who choose to become young scholars ahead of their high school peers. Visit our campus on Discovery Day and get to know the students and faculty. If being part of a community of younger scholars appeals to a student, [he or she] should take the initiative to apply and spend time preparing an application [that] will demonstrate what kind of learner [he or she is] and aspires to become.

—*Dr. Mary Marcy, Vice President*
and Provost of Simon's Rock College

Sit in some college classes and get a feel for the pace and how testing is done. Remember that there are no worksheets to fill in. Learn how to study in-depth, not relying on short-term memory. Master the material!

—*Dr. Richard J. Sinclair, Dean of TAMS*

First, acquire all the information possible on what the TAMS experience is like by attending our preview days, spend-a-day program, and talking to current and past TAMS students. Then, be sure and let our experienced staff answer any questions or address any concerns you might have to make sure that you have accurate information. And finally, recognize that being somewhat nervous about taking on a new challenge is perfectly normal because anytime we move out of our comfort zone this occurs.

—*Dr. Donna Fleming, Director of Counseling and Research, TAMS*

Advice for Parents From Parents

Parents of early entrants who attend special programs and parents of those who have pursued early college on their own were asked: What advice can you offer parents of prospective early entrants?

Remember that you are supporting your child in one important decision—one that can be adjusted in a variety of ways if it isn't working out as hoped! This is for the benefit of your child—not for appearances—and if your child wants to return to high school, or change colleges, or change majors, or . . .—you are seeking the optimal placement for your child at this time in his or her life; you can seek advice, engage in discussions, and continue to seek the best options if necessary.

Be aware that this is going to feel wrong at times. And, others will definitely let you know that you're making a mistake. You never thought you'd be "losing" a child so early—we hear about the dynamics of empty nests when children hit 18 and move out—but this is happening to you long before you thought it would—and you'll second guess yourself every time your child is unhappy or confused. But, it's likely that your child was unhappy and confused in high school to have considered this option—adolescents are unhappy and confused almost by definition—early entrance to college isn't a cure—it's a step along the way.

197

Support your child and his or her decisions as he tries to maneuver through this new academic and social environment. Encourage decision making rather than making decisions on his or her behalf. Remember that this entrance into the larger world really does open up the world to independent thinking—thinking that may challenge your values—but this is a stage through which your child has to pass, even if he or she is only 17, or 16, or 15—and (s)he needs to come through this stage more confident in his or her ability to become a successful adult.

Do not get tempted with saving a year or two. Ensure your child is mature and can adjust socially and is prepared psychologically to handle the pressures of college and peer pressure.

Carefully consider it. Do a cost/benefit analysis (emotionally, socially, and academically). Take advantage of decision support that is available. I would tell parents to take a class in parenting gifted/talented kids, if you haven't already. Have your child do above-grade-level testing.

Do it! But, experiment first with some time on campus (classes, extracurriculars, working in a lab, etc.). Think through what the benefits will be and what the negatives could be. Talk extensively with faculty and the advising people to see what they think and how they suggest your child proceed. Think about both the academic side and social side. Investigate money issues early. Early entrants may have special issues getting loans and some scholarships. Be aware that your child will be competing with older students for both admission and money. Age will be seen as a risk factor for both, not as an advantage.

Success in college requires not only academic talent and skills, but also social and emotional maturity. Parents know their children best. It is our responsibility to guide them and present them with many possibilities for success. The final decision, however, still belongs to our children.

Let the student make the decision. All of my daughter's higher education is her decision. I didn't even lift a pen or make any calls. She filled out the forms and I signed and pay for her education. Nothing more.

Be supportive of your child. Let it be [his or her] choice, not yours, as your child is the one who will be away at college—not you and I. Listen; if [he or she isn't] feeling well, find out why. Remind [him or her] that there is a campus health center and not [to] be afraid or ashamed to use it regardless. Keep in contact. It is much easier now with cell phones and e-mail than ever before. [He or she] may not like it. But, you will feel better and so will [he or she] even if [he or she doesn't] admit it to you. If your child changes his or her mind, let that be OK too. This is less likely to occur if it is the child's choice instead of the parents' choice.

Know your child and what kind of environment he or she operates in most effectively.

Do not pressure your child to enter the program.

If your student is happy in high school, doing well, and is challenged, don't change (unless the child is mature enough to continue academic success and really wants to go). Remember . . . college can be great and poor at the same time. You will find very poor professors/teachers at college, too. Early entrance programs do not provide much additional chutzpah to a résumé for top national colleges. At some schools, it may be a negative for acceptance.

Bright and talented students often spend their summers traveling or doing extra classes, enrichment, etc., which is well and good, but they also need the practical side of holding a job, balancing a checkbook, learning to cook, clean, and do laundry before they are ready to leave home. It can be hard to let go of being involved with every decision your child makes, but letting go forces [him or her] or gives [him or her] the chance to make decisions and take responsibility, and therefore become an adult. We have to trust we taught them well growing up and then let them go to fulfill their purpose.

Do not utilize your past experiences to determine the future success of your child. Afford [him or her] the opportunity to explore [his or her] views, opinions, and most of all, [his or her] ability to make choices through [his or her] educational journeys.

You need to know that your child can take care of him- or herself without you there. Also, be prepared for the emotional "empty nest" stage that parents must face. Kids need encouragement and praise for their accomplishments, so try to not share too much of your grief in letting them leave home earlier than expected. Teenagers need their space to function independently in this situation, and they will learn from their mistakes on their own, so it's better to not criticize troubles they may encounter. And, if they want to enter college early, it should only be their decision. Have them complete all of the applications.

It is necessary to be able to communicate with your child, but also give him or her space. You must trust your child.

Advice for Prospective Radical Accelerants and Their Parents From Gifted-Child Experts

Some of the leading experts in the field of gifted education who have expertise with radical accelerants were asked to respond to the following questions: What advice can you offer to prospective students and their parents who are considering *radical acceleration*? What considerations must they factor more heavily into their decision that may not be as critical for students who are entering college only 1 or 2 years early?

By definition, radical accelerants have had less life experience, [that is], fewer years to learn and to mature, than students who enter college at the typical age or just a year or two early. Whether this will present a problem for these students depends on the extent to which they are prepared academically, socially, and emotionally for the particular college setting in which they will be placed.

Clearly, radical accelerants must be very bright and quick to absorb new material to be successful in college at such a young age, but that's not enough. Study skills and content knowledge will also be critical for students to excel in rigorous college courses. Good social skills will be important for them to interact, not only with older peers, but also with faculty, and emotional maturity and independence will be important in dealing with such aspects of daily living as handling money, doing laundry, etc.

Students who skipped several years of schooling early in their careers but who completed a high school program with seniors are more likely to be better prepared in many of these aspects than those who are considering entering college after eight or ninth grade. Radical accelerants who have not completed high school may be better served by enrolling in an early entrance program that offers academic and social support for young college students or by selecting a less competitive college setting where most entering students have not taken a full spectrum of AP courses. Commuting from home to college, at least at first, may be an option for radical accelerants not ready to live on their own.

Students considering radical acceleration should evaluate their own readiness for college in all of these aspects and then evaluate the appropriate college setting in which they are likely to succeed. If they have doubts about the likelihood of their success or if they have to make compromises they don't want to make, such as attending a less competitive college or commuting, they should probably wait another year or two and then reevaluate their readiness. If, on the other hand, they have the level of content knowledge, study skills, social adjustment, and emotional maturity that the college setting they have chosen requires, they are likely to be successful.

201

—Dr. Linda Brody, Director of the Julian C. Stanley Study of
Exceptional Talent (SET), Center for Talented Youth, Johns Hopkins
University, Baltimore, MD

Radical acceleration is a pretty radical move! It's a decision that mustn't be taken lightly. If you are planning to enter college 3 or more years earlier than usual, you are doing something highly unusual and therefore it must be in response to a situation that is highly unusual.

A vitally important element of this is the ability level of the student who is considering radical acceleration. In my view, it is not an intervention suited to moderately gifted students. While many gifted students could handle more moderate forms of acceleration, such as subject acceleration or a single grade skip, young people who would benefit academically, socially, and emotionally from radical acceleration appear in the population only rarely; probably fewer than 1 person in 1,000. In terms of intellectual ability we would be looking at an IQ of at least 145.

Of course, intellectual ability isn't the only consideration. Radical accelerants' emotional maturity is even more important—indeed much more important—than it would be for someone undertaking a single grade skip. Hobbies and interests are also important. A 9-year-old in a class of 12-year-olds is not going to find easy acceptance if the books he likes reading and the games he likes playing are what his classmates enjoyed 3 years ago.

A few years ago, a colleague and I developed an annotated bibliography of the international research on radical acceleration (Gross & Van Vliet, 2003). [The factors below seem] to be related to successful radical acceleration.

Personal characteristics of the student. It is important that radical accelerants are strongly motivated to achieve, demonstrate persistence in striving after goals, and are passionate about learning in at least one subject area. It also helps for students to have acquired advanced study skills. They should also have attained results on achievement tests that are at least average for the group of students they will join. It can come as a bit of a culture shock for students who have excelled academically to suddenly find themselves performing at the average level of their new class!

Involving the student in educational planning. Positive outcomes ensue when students are strongly supportive of the educational strategies that are employed. Students who are considering radically accelerating into college should think carefully to ensure that the benefits they will acquire will outweigh any regrets about missed high school opportunities, such as editing the school newspaper, joining musical groups, competing in academic and sporting competitions, going to the prom, being valedictorian at graduation, or applying for college and university scholarships. Students who excel in athletics should realize that, after radical acceleration, they may no longer be able to participate in competitive sports at school or college.

Supportive family. It appears to be particularly important for students to know that their parents are truly their partners in the acceleration process. Encouragement and support from people who are important to us have been shown to have important positive effects for students who radically accelerate. Parents must also be willing to allow their children increased independence despite their young age! A mom who is bewailing the empty nest may cause quite severe feelings of guilt in the gifted son or daughter who is, necessarily, loosening the childhood ties somewhat—an essential element in growing up. Parents must accept that leaving home to go to college does not mean a decrease in their son or daughter's love and affection but rather a change in the ways in which it is expressed. Parental support appears to be dependent on parents being informed about the process of radical acceleration and educational counseling for parents has been shown to facilitate radical acceleration.

Supportive educators. Successful radical acceleration commonly involves at least one educator who is knowledgeable about the needs of gifted children. Case studies reveal the important role this educator plays as [a] long-term critical planner, monitor, and mentor—identifying appropriate interventions for the student, providing information concerning access to these interventions, and supporting the student, [his or her] families, and [his or her] teachers.

Individualized acceleration planning. Students need to have access to a variety of acceleration options so that they can choose the combination of options most suited to their circumstances. Julian Stanley (1979) called it a smorgasbord of options. That creates such a lovely image of gifted students choosing, from that smorgasbord, options that will best meet their academic and social needs. These can include early school entry, subject acceleration, grade skipping, concurrent enrollment in school and university or college, curriculum compacting, curriculum telescoping, Advanced Placement courses, part-time college courses, summer programs, and correspondence courses. It appears important to consider the timing of implementation of such strategies, as appropriateness of timing will differ between students depending on their cognitive and affective needs.

A flexible approach to teaching and learning. Radical acceleration works best when there is flexible curriculum planning based on individual needs. Educators need to ensure that students are able to access a wide variety of enrichment and acceleration options. Planning needs to allow for regular readjustment of the educational program, as students' needs and circumstances change.

Programming to support the affective needs of students. Program modifications supporting successful radical acceleration should include provisions to address the affective needs of gifted students. It seems important to pay particular attention to the need for interaction with peers sharing similar levels of intellectual ability. Provision for counseling before and during the process of radical acceleration has been shown to support positive academic and affective outcomes.

Opportunities to develop skills for advanced study. Students who decide to radically accelerate appear to benefit from involvement in Advanced Placement courses and part-time enrollment in college or university. Previous experience of subject or grade advancement also seems beneficial. Such experience provides students with the opportunity to develop the skills necessary for effective note taking, essay writing, and time-management.

—Professor Miraca U. M. Gross, Director, Gifted Education Research, Resource and Information Centre (GERRIC), The University of New South Wales, Sydney, Australia

Radical acceleration most often occurs in steps, or single grade skips over the years, that then result in being several grades ahead of age peers by the end of the traditional K–12 continuum. Approach the decision to accelerate in a thoughtful manner that honors what the student wants to experience. This includes actively generating a list of pros and cons with the student. Ideally, this list is dynamic, in that it changes as often as new information is available. This list helps everyone involved realize that there is not one perfect solution. Rather, there are options to consider that possess relative strengths and weaknesses. Communication between parent(s) and student is vital, as the student will benefit from having the solid foundation of a supportive relationship when encountering unexpected aspects of multiple grade skips. Similar recommendations are reasonable for students entering college 1 or 2 years early. However, the support and flexible thinking of trusted adults is vital to those students who are truly experiencing what they feel to be uncharted waters entering full-time college as a significantly younger student.

—Ms. Colleen Harsin, Director of Services, Davidson Institute
for Talent Development, Reno, NV

Basically, students just have to be extra mature and organized—and even more exceptionally bright. Radical acceleration also demands a little more of boys than girls, in the sense that they are a bit less likely to make friends among the regular-age college students, particularly girls. Many male accelerants are quite content with that and begin to date when they are upper classmen or graduate students.

—Dr. Nancy Robinson, Professor Emerita of Psychiatry and
Behavioral Sciences, and cofounder of The Halbert and Nancy
Robinson Center for Young Scholars, University of Washington,
Seattle, WA

Advice for Parents, High School Teachers, and Guidance Counselors From Early Entrance Program Administrators

Program directors were asked: How can parents, high school teachers, and guidance counselors help young entrants prepare for the academic, social, and emotional demands of college?

This is a loaded question and I don't know where to begin. With politics? The politics of education, race, class, etc.? With stereotypes? Eliminate the prejudices and preconceptions of (some of) those people? Cynicism aside, high schools should provide greater academic rigor for all students, not just gifted students, to the degree that they can handle. Acceleration and acceleration options would ideally be discussed and not looked upon with suspicion. With encouragement, but not to the point where it becomes painful—[schools will have] that perfect balance between pushing and allowing that is difficult to find. Write, write, and write some more. Talk about plagiarism and academic integrity. Learn what the options are. Listen to them. Love them.

—*Ms. Susan Colgate, Director of AAG*

We need to encourage students to take rigorous courses. Find balance with an emphasis on academics. Parents can encourage and nurture independent study habits and responsible social choices. Encourage students to enroll in one to two college courses the year before early entry. Have an open dialogue about social issues.

—*Mr. Shailindar Singh, Interim Head of the Clarkson School*

A great question, but one that is difficult for me to answer as most traditional secondary school teachers and educators do not agree with accelerated efforts and those that do often help by referring students to an EEP-type effort. They can, at the very least, be understanding and sensitive to the special needs of the highly gifted and not believe (and fight against) the social stereotype that gifted students do not need nurturing, care, and support.

—*Mr. Richard Maddox, Director of EEP at CSULA*

Offer gifted and honors classes, teach good study habits and time management, and instill good work ethics.

—*Ms. Lisa Whitaker, Director of GAMES*

Help the student take a good comprehensive look at all the issues. I have found that the more a student thinks about and discusses the issues, the more likely entering early (or not) will be the correct decision.

—*Dr. Nicholas Colangelo,*
Director of the Belin-Blank Center and NAASE

Academically—have them take as many AP-like classes as possible; socially—make sure they don't leave a serious relationship behind. Have them bring closure; emotionally—help them to develop organizational skills and self-discipline in the face of much freedom.

—*Dr. Susan Assouline,*
Associate Director of the Belin-Blank Center and NAASE

207

[Parents, teachers, and guidance counselors] can encourage students to seek new challenges and to take risks . . . to not fear change and forging new paths. They can nurture gifts and talents from an early age and help students trust and value their special abilities. Helping students to feel confident in their abilities is critical for success in so many ways.

—*Dr. Elizabeth Connell, Director of PEG*

Parents should be aware of what their child can handle academically and socially, yet they should allow their child the freedom to excel on [his or her] own, to make [his or her] own choices, and they should encourage [their child] to do so. Encouragement without excessive coddling or forcing a specific path is important. Students should be prepared to live on their own, making their own academic and personal decisions. High school teachers and guidance counselors should be sure that students are able to study independently and that they have a genuine love of learning.

—*Dr. Pennelope Von Helmolt, Director of RHP*

They can learn as much as possible about early college and how it reflects college life and in what ways it may differ. There are many different approaches to early college education, and it is important for parents, teachers, and counselors alike to understand the differences and to choose the best fit for the particular student. The learning communities of early college have cultures that are particular to their identities and locations. Simon's Rock College offers a liberal arts curriculum that promotes critical thinking. Other programs may focus on career preparation. Costs differ, as does the value of the education. It is important to understand the available student support services and learning opportunities outside of the classroom.

—*Dr. Mary Marcy, Vice President and Provost of Simon's Rock College*

Parents should gradually allow more independence, with the realization that the student may need to suffer some consequences for failing to be responsible. Send them to summer programs that require them to live with another person.

Teachers and counselors need to constantly remind the students that they are moving up another level and will now be on at least an equal footing with their new classmates. Stop telling them they are so smart. This can lead to shattering experiences.

These programs may not be the best choice for those who are focused on one particular college (MIT, etc.). It is difficult to be the top student and disappointment may follow.

—*Dr. Richard J. Sinclair, Dean of TAMS*

For the academic demands, students need to be encouraged to learn how to apply the information they are learning, and they need to be evaluated not just by how well they have memorized rote information. They also need to be encouraged to challenge themselves by taking the most advanced classes in all academic realms such as math, science, history, English, [and] foreign languages. Parents can help them get involved in an outside activity that requires diligence and mastery such as music or sports. Students would also benefit from involvement in community service and spiritual activities that encourage them to develop a strong sense of their own morals and values. Parents can also help by providing increasing levels of independence for students and opportunities to make choices and decisions in a safe and structured environment.

—*Dr. Donna Fleming, Director of Counseling and Research, TAMS*

Conclusion

209

Well, there you have it. The bottom line is that early entrance is a fine option for students who are motivated and ready academically, socially, and emotionally. It is not, however, a panacea for underachievement. There is no magic wand, no miracle cure for intellectually gifted underachievers who think something external to them (e.g., challenging college-level coursework) is going to make all the difference. If it does, I would argue that these students have internalized the desire to reverse their underachievement by taking some positive action. Whether conscious of it or not, people must be willing participants in their own lives to allow change.

After reading the unique viewpoints of so many people, my hope is that you have extracted the information that will be most helpful to you. That's all that really matters. Writing this book has been a truly rewarding experience, mainly because I have had the opportunity to learn so much from all of the contributors. I hope you have, too.

References

Advanced Academy of Georgia. (2002). *Benefits of the academy*. Retrieved July 20, 2006, from http://www.advanced academy.org/benefits.htm

Barnett, L. B., Albert, M. E., & Brody, L. E. (2005). The Center for Talented Youth talent search and academic programs. *High Ability Studies, 16*(1), 27–40.

Brody, L. E. (2005). The Study of Exceptional Talent. *High Ability Studies, 16*(1), 87–96.

Brody, L. E., & Blackburn, C. C. (1996). Nurturing exceptional talent: SET as a legacy of SMPY. In C. P. Benbow & D. Lubinski (Eds.), *Intellectual talent: Psychometric and social issues* (pp. 246–265). Baltimore: The Johns Hopkins University Press.

Brody, L. E., & Mills, C. J. (2005). Talent search research: What have we learned? *High Ability Studies, 16*(1), 97–111.

Brody, L. E., Muratori, M. C., & Stanley, J. C. (2004). Early entrance to college: Academic, social, and emotional considerations. In N. Colangelo, S. G. Assouline, & M. U. M. Gross (Eds.), *A nation deceived: How schools hold back America's brightest students* (Vol. 2, pp. 97–107). Iowa City, IA: The Connie Belin & Jacqueline N. Blank International Center for Gifted Education and Talent Development.

Brody, L. E., & Stanley, J. C. (1991). Young college entrants: Assessing factors that contribute to success. In W. T. Southern & E. D. Jones (Eds.), *Academic acceleration of gifted children* (pp. 102–132). New York: Teachers College Press.

Campbell, D. T., & Stanley, J. C. (1966). *Experimental and quasi-experimental designs for research.* Chicago, IL: Rand McNally.

Claremont Colleges. (n.d.). *Welcome to the Claremont Colleges.* Retrieved July 27, 2006, from http://www.claremont.edu

Clarkson University. (2005a). *Frequently asked questions.* Retrieved July 20, 2006, from http://www.clarkson.edu/tcs/faq.html

Clarkson University. (2005b). *The Clarkson school.* Retrieved July 20, 2006, from http://www.clarkson.edu/tcs/academics.html

Colangelo, N. (2006, April 6). *UI center to research academic acceleration with $1.95 million grant.* University of Iowa News Release.

Colangelo, N., Assouline, S. G., & Gross, M. U. M. (Eds.). (2004). *A nation deceived: How schools hold back America's brightest students* (Vol. 1). Iowa City, IA: The Connie Belin & Jacqueline N. Blank International Center for Gifted Education and Talent Development.

Early Entrance Program. (2004). *EEP description packet: A brief description and history.* Retrieved July 20, 2006, from http://www.calstatela.edu/academic/eep

Fischer, J. (1990, April 1). 13-year-old math whiz Lenny Ng of Chapel Hill may be the smartest kid in America. *Charlotte Observer,* 1E–2E.

Gerdes, H., & Mallinckrodt, B. (1994). Emotional, social, and academic adjustment of college students: A longitudinal study of retention. *Journal of Counseling & Development, 72,* 281–288.

Georgia Academy of Mathematics, Engineering, & Science. (2006). *Information.* Retrieved July 20, 2006, from http://www.mgc.edu/academic/scimathbus/games/info.cfm

Gross, M. U. M., & Van Vliet, H. (2003). *Radical acceleration of highly gifted children: An annotated bibliography of international research on highly gifted young people who graduate from high school three or more years early.* Sydney, Australia: Gifted Education Research, Resource and Information Centre.

Halbert and Nancy Robinson Center for Young Scholars. (2005). *Early entrance program.* Retrieved July 20, 2006, from http://depts.washington.edu/CSCY/program/earlyentrance

Hoftyzer, R. (2001). Redeeming the time. *Vision: News from the Connie Belin & Jacqueline N. Blank Center for Gifted Education and Talent Development, 9*(2), 12.

Karnes, F. A., & Riley, T. L. (2005). *Competitions for talented kids: Win scholarships, big prize money, and recognition.* Waco, TX: Prufrock Press.

Kett, J. (1974). History of age grouping in America. In J. S. Coleman (Ed.), *Youth: Transition to adulthood. A report of the Panel on Youth of the President's Science Advisory Committee* (pp. 6–29; Publication No. 4106-00037). Washington, DC: U.S. Government Printing Office.

Lupkowski, A. E., & Assouline, S. G. (1992). *Jane and Johnny love math: Recognizing and encouraging mathematical talent in elementary students: A guidebook for parents* (3rd ed.). New York: Royal Fireworks Press.

Lupkowski-Shoplik, A. E., Benbow, C. P., Assouline, S. G., & Brody, L. E. (2003). Talent searches: Meeting the needs of academically talented youth. In N. Colangelo & G. A. Davis (Eds.), *Handbook of gifted education* (3rd ed., pp. 204–218). Boston: Allyn & Bacon.

Marland, S. P., Jr. (1972). Education of the gifted and talented: Report to the Congress of the United States by the U.S. Commissioner of Education and background papers submitted to the U.S. Office of Education, 2 vols. Washington, DC: U.S. Government Printing Office. (Government Documents, Y4.L 11/2: G36)

Mathews, J. (2003). *Harvard schmarvard: Getting beyond the Ivy League to the college that is best for you.* New York: Three Rivers Press.

Mathis, M., & Lecci, L. (1999). Hardiness and college adjustment: Identifying students in need of services. *Journal of College Student Development, 40,* 305–309.

Mooney, S. P., Sherman, M. F., & Lo Presto, C. T. (1991). Academic locus of control, self-esteem, and perceived distance from home as predictors of college adjustment. *Journal of Counseling and Development, 69,* 445–448.

Mount Holyoke College. (n.d.). *The five college consortium.* Retrieved July 26, 2006, from http://www.mtholyoke.edu/acad/5college.shtml

Muratori, M. (2006). Study skills: Don't leave home without them. *Imagine . . . Opportunities and Resources for Academically Talented Youth, 13*(4), 31.

Muratori, M., Colangelo, N., & Assouline, S. (2003). Early entrance students: Impressions of their first semester of college. *Gifted Child Quarterly, 47,* 219–238.

213

Muratori, M., Stanley, J. C., Gross, M. U. M., Ng, L., Tao, T., Ng, J, et al. (2006). Insights from SMPY's greatest former child prodigies: Drs. Terence ("Terry") Tao and Lenhard ("Lenny") Ng reflect on their talent development. *Gifted Child Quarterly, 50,* 307–324.

Muratori, M. C. (2003). *A multiple case study examining the adjustment of ten early entrants.* Unpublished doctoral dissertation, The University of Iowa, Iowa City, IA.

Muratori, M. C. (2004, May). *SET members' impressions of their high school experiences.* Paper presented at the Seventh Biennial Henry B. & Jocelyn Wallace National Research Symposium on Talent Development, The University of Iowa, Iowa City.

Olszewski-Kubilius, P. (1995). A summary of research regarding early entrance to college. *Roeper Review, 18,* 121–126.

Olszewski-Kubilius, P. (1998). Early entrance to college: Students' stories. *Journal of Secondary Gifted Education, 10,* 226–247.

Olszewski-Kubilius, P. (2003). Special summer and Saturday programs for gifted students. In N. Colangelo & G. A. Davis (Eds.), *Handbook of gifted education* (3rd ed., pp. 219–228). Boston: Allyn & Bacon.

Olszewski-Kubilius, P. (2004). Talent searches and accelerated programming for gifted students. In N. Colangelo, S. G. Assouline, & M. U. M. Gross (Eds.), *A nation deceived: How schools hold back America's brightest students* (Vol. 2, pp. 69–76). Iowa City, IA: The Connie Belin & Jacqueline N. Blank International Center for Gifted Education and Talent Development.

Olszewski-Kubilius, P. (2005). The Center for Talent Development at Northwestern University: An example of replication and reformation. *High Ability Studies, 16*(1), 55–69.

Pressey, S. L. (1949). *Educational acceleration: Appraisal and basic problems* (Bureau of Educational Research Monographs, No. 31). Columbus: Ohio State University Press.

Program for the Exceptionally Gifted. (n.d.a). *Admission to the Program for the Exceptionally Gifted (PEG).* Retrieved July 20, 2006, from http://www.mbc.edu/admission/admit_peg.asp

Program for the Exceptionally Gifted. (n.d.b). *PEG residence life.* Retrieved July 20, 2006, from http://www.mbc.edu/peg/pegreslife.asp

Resident Honors Program. (n.d.). *Program information.* Retrieved July 26, 2006, from http://www.usc.edu/dept/LAS/general_studies/RHP/moreinfo.htm

Robinson, N. M., & Noble, K. D. (1992). Acceleration: Valuable high school to college options. *Gifted Child Today, 15*(2), 20–23.

Schlossberg, N. K., Lynch, A. Q., & Chickering, A. W. (1989). *Improving higher education environments for adults: Responsive programs and services from entry to departure.* San Francisco: Jossey-Bass.

Simon's Rock College of Bard. (2006a). *Academics.* Retrieved July 26, 2006, from http://www.simons-rock.edu/academics

Simon's Rock College of Bard. (2006b). *For parents and educators.* Retrieved July 26, 2006, from http://www.simons-rock.edu/parents

Stanley, J. C. (1979). The study and facilitation of talent for mathematics. In A. H. Passow (Ed.), *The gifted and the talented: Their education and development. The seventy-eighth yearbook of the National Society for the Study of Education* (pp. 169–185). Chicago: University of Chicago Press.

Stanley, J. C. (1996). In the beginning: The Study of Mathematically Precocious Youth. In C. P. Benbow & D. Lubinski (Eds.), *Intellectual talent: Psychometric and social issues* (pp. 225–235). Baltimore: Johns Hopkins University Press.

Stanley, J. C. (2005). A quiet revolution: Finding boys and girls who reason exceptionally well mathematically and/or verbally and helping them get the supplemental educational opportunities they need. *High Ability Studies, 16*(1), 5–14.

Stanley, J. C., & Benbow, C. P. (1982). Educating mathematically precocious youths: Twelve policy recommendations. *Educational Researcher, 11*(5), 4–9.

Texas Academy of Mathematics and Science. (n.d.a). *Frequently asked questions.* Retrieved July 26, 2006, from http://www.tams.unt.edu/admission/admission_faq.shtml

Texas Academy of Mathematics and Science. (n.d.b). *Overview.* Retrieved July 26, 2006, from http://www.tams.unt.edu/academics/academics_program.shtml

Tourón, J. (Ed.). (2005). Special issue: The Center for Talented Youth model. *High Ability Studies, 16*(1).

U.S. Department of Education. (2006). *National Mathematics Advisory Panel: Strengthening math education through research.* Retrieved July 18, 2006, from http://www.ed.gov/about/bdscomm/list/mathpanel/factsheet.html

Viadero, D. (2001). U.S. urged to rethink high school: Senior year is often dead end, panel says. *Education Week, 20*(19), 1–12.

Waits, T., Setzer, J. C., & Lewis, L. (2005). *Dual credit and exam-based courses in U.S. public high schools: 2002–03* (NCES 2005-009). Washington, DC: U.S. Department of Education, National Center for Education Statistics.

Appendix: Selected Resources

Academically Challenging Opportunities for Middle School and High School Students

Useful Web Sites

Academic Competitions
http://cty.jhu.edu/imagine/links.html
Find links to many academic competitions on the
Center for Talented Youth's Web site.

Academic Summer Programs
http://cty.jhu.edu/imagine/links.html
Find links to academic summer programs on the Center
for Talented Youth's Web site.

Advanced Placement (AP)
http://www.collegeboard.com/student/testing/ap/
about.html

This site provides information for students and parents about the Advanced Placement program and exams.

Distance Education
http://cty.jhu.edu/imagine/links.html
Find links to distance education programs on the Center for Talented Youth's Web site.

International Baccalaureate (IB)
http://www.ibo.org
The official Web site of the International Baccalaureate Organization provides information about its three programs of international education (primary school, middle school, and diploma programs).

Study Abroad Programs
http://www.aifs.com
The American Institute for Foreign Study offers international education, travel, and cultural exchange programs for high school and college students.

http://www.studyabroad.com
This site offers a comprehensive directory of study abroad programs.

Early Entrance Programs Contact Information

Academy of Young Scholars: University of Washington
Robinson Center for Young Scholars
University of Washington
Guthrie Annex 2
Box 351630
Seattle, WA 98195-1630
Phone: 206-543-4160
E-mail: cscy@u.washington.edu
http://depts.washington.edu/cscy/programs/earlyentrance

Advanced Academy of Georgia (AAG):
State University of West Georgia
State University of West Georgia
Honors House
Carrollton, GA 30118
Phone: 678-839-6249
E-mail: afinch@westga.edu
http://www.advancedacademy.org

Bard High School Early College (BHSEC)
Bard High School Early College
525 East Houston Street
New York, NY 10002
Phone: 212-995-8479
E-mail: bhsec@bard.edu
http://www.bard.edu/bhsec

Boston University Academy (BUA): Boston University
Boston University Academy
One University Road
Boston, MA 02215
Phone: 617-353-9000
E-mail: admissions@buacademy.org,
operations@buacademy.org
http://www.buacademy.org

Clarkson School: Clarkson University
The Clarkson School
Clarkson University
P.O. Box 5650
Potsdam, New York 13699-5650
Phone: 315-268-6400; 800-527-6577
E-mail: tcs@clarkson.edu
http://www.clarkson.edu/tcs

Davidson Academy of Nevada: University of Nevada, Reno
The Davidson Academy of Nevada
1670 North Virginia St., 2nd Floor
Reno, NV 89557
Phone: 775-337-0171
E-mail: admin@DavidsonAcademyNevada.org
http://www.davidsonacademy.unr.edu

Early Entrance Program (EEP):
California State University, Los Angeles
Early Entrance Program
California State University Los Angeles
Fine Arts 218
Los Angeles, CA 90032
Phone: 323-343-2287
E-mail: rmaddox@calstatela.edu
http://www.calstatela.edu/academic/eep

Early Entrance Program/Transition School (EEP/TS):
University of Washington
Robinson Center for Young Scholars
University of Washington
Guthrie Annex 2
Box 351630
Seattle, WA 98195-1630
Phone: 206-543-4160
E-mail: cscy@u.washington.edu
http://depts.washington.edu/cscy/programs/earlyentrance

Early Honors Program (EHP): Alaska Pacific University
Alaska Pacific University
Office of Admissions
4101 University Drive
Anchorage, AK 99508
Phone: 907-564-8248; 800-252-7528
E-mail: admissions@alaskapacific.edu
http://www.alaskapacific.edu

Georgia Academy of Math, Engineering, and Science (GAMES):
Middle Georgia College
GAMES
Middle Georgia College
1100 Second Street, SE
Cochran, GA 31014
Phone: 478-934-3471
E-mail: games@mgc.edu
http://web2.mgc.edu/natsci/games/gameshome.html

*Kentucky Academy of Mathematics and Science: Western Kentucky
University* (effective fall 2007, based on TAMS model)
The Center for Gifted Studies
Western Kentucky University
1906 College Heights Blvd. #71031
Bowling Green, KY 42101-1031
Phone: 270-745-6323
E-mail: academy@wku.edu
http://www.wku.edu/academy

Missouri Academy of Science, Mathematics and Computing
(MASMC): Northwest Missouri State University
MASMC
Northwest Missouri State University
Office of Enrollment
800 University Drive
Maryville, MO 64468
Phone: 660-562-1060; 877-398-4615
E-mail: MASMC@nwmissouri.edu
http://www.nwmissouri.edu/MASMC

National Academy of Arts, Sciences, and Engineering (NAASE): The University of Iowa
The Connie Belin & Jacqueline N. Blank International Center for Gifted Education and Talent Development (Belin-Blank Center)
The University of Iowa
600 Blank Honors Center
Iowa City, IA 52242
Phone: 319-335-6148; 800-336-6463
E-mail: belinblank@uiowa.edu
http://www.education.uiowa.edu/belinblank/programs/naase

Program for the Exceptionally Gifted (PEG): Mary Baldwin College
Program for the Exceptionally Gifted
Mary Baldwin College
Staunton, VA 24401
Phone: 540-887-7019
E-mail: peg@mbc.edu
http://www.mbc.edu/peg

Resident Honors Program (RHP): University of Southern California
Resident Honors Program
University of Southern California
3454 Trousdale Parkway, CAS 200
Los Angeles, CA 90089
Phone: 213-740-2961; 800-USC-2961
http://www.usc.edu/rhp

Shimer College
Shimer College
Early Entrant Program
3424 South State Street
Chicago, IL 60616-3893
Phone: 312-335-3500
E-mail: wdapp@shimer.edu, cassie@shimer.edu
http://www.shimer.edu/admissions/earlyent.html

Simon's Rock College (SRC)
Simon's Rock College of Bard
84 East Alford Road
Great Barrington, MA 01230
Phone: 413-528-0771; 800-235-7186
E-mail: admit@simons-rock.edu
http://www.simons-rock.edu

Texas Academy of Leadership in the Humanities (TALH):
Lamar University
Texas Academy of Leadership in the Humanities
Lamar University
P.O. Box 10062
Beaumont, TX 77710
Phone: 409-839-2995
E-mail: talh@hal.lamar.edu
http://dept.lamar.edu/taolith

Texas Academy of Mathematics and Science (TAMS):
University of North Texas
P.O. Box 305309
University of North Texas
Denton, TX 76203-5309
Phone: 800-241-TAMS
E-mail: admissions@tams.sch.unt.edu
http://www.tams.unt.edu

Early Entrance General Resources

Useful Web Sites

http://www.ditd.org
The Davidson Institute for Talent Development has developed student and parent versions of a guidebook on early entrance that can be downloaded.

http://www.earlyentrance.org
This Web site is dedicated exclusively to early college entrance and provides information about early entrance programs.

http://www.jhu.edu/cty/imagine/links.html
Find links to information about early college entrance on the Center for Talented Youth's Web site.

http://www.earlyentrancefoundation.org
The Early Entrance Foundation was established in 2004 as a nonprofit organization to assist profoundly gifted students who are ready for early college entrance by providing them with support, guidance, and counseling.

Financial Aid and Scholarships

Useful Web Sites

http://www.ed.gov
The U.S. Department of Education's official Web site provides information for students, parents, and educators

about legislation related to education, financial aid, grants, and the like.

http://www.finaid.org
This Web site is an outstanding resource for those in search of financial aid.

http://www.jackkentcookefoundation.org
The JKC Foundation provides a limited number of scholarships to academically talented high school, college, and graduate students who demonstrate financial need.

http://www.jhu.edu/cty/imagine/links.html
Find links to many Web resources that provide information about scholarships and financial aid under the College Search and Application link.

http://www.nationalmerit.org
The official Web site of the National Merit Scholarship Corporation offers information about its two undergraduate scholarship programs.

General College Admissions/ College Planning

Selected Books and Magazines

Berger, S. L. (2006). *College planning for gifted students.* Waco, TX: Prufrock Press.

Hartman, M. (Ed.). *Imagine… Opportunities and resources for academically talented youth.* Baltimore: Johns Hopkins University Center for Talented Youth. (Published five times a year.)

Hughes, C. (2003). *What it really takes to get into the Ivy League & other highly selective colleges.* New York: McGraw-Hill.

Mathews, J. (2003). *Harvard schmarvard: Getting beyond the Ivy League to the college that is best for you.* New York: Three Rivers Press.

Montauk, R., & Klein, K. (2000). *How to get into the top colleges.* New York: Prentice Hall.

Springer, S. P., & Franck, M. R. (2005). *Admission matters: What students and parents need to know about getting into college.* San Francisco: Jossey-Bass.

Useful Web Sites

http://www.collegeboard.com
The official College Board Web site provides information about college success and planning, as well as its standardized tests (e.g., the SAT, PSAT, and Advanced Placement exams)

http://www.jhu.edu/cty/imagine/links.html
Find links to many Web resources that will aid in the college search and application processes. Also, find links to career exploration sites and the professional associations of many academic disciplines.

General Resources for the Gifted and Talented (G/T)

Useful Web Sites

http://cty.jhu.edu/imagine/links.html
Find links to many G/T resources on the Center for Talented Youth's Web site.

http://www.gt-cybersource.org
The Davidson Institute for Talent Development offers a gateway to resources for gifted and talented students.

http://www.hoagiesgifted.org
This comprehensive site offers many types of resources for gifted students, their parents, and educators.

http://www.nationdeceived.org
Download a copy of *A Nation Deceived: How Schools Hold Back America's Brightest Students*, the Templeton National Report on Acceleration.

http://www.nagc.org
The official Web site of the National Association for Gifted Children provides information about the organization's annual conference, as well as resources for gifted students, parents, and educators.

http://www.sengifted.org
An organization devoted to the social/emotional development of academically talented students, Supporting Emotional Needs of the Gifted (SENG) provides parents with access to articles, information about SENG parent groups, and many other resources.

http://www.gifted.uconn.edu/nrcgt.html
The National Research Center on the Gifted and Talented (NRC/GT), which is housed in the University of Connecticut's Neag Center for Gifted Education & Talent Development, provides access to online resources, the NRC/GT newsletter, research-based resources, and educational resource links.

Talent Search Centers (United States)

Academic Talent Search (ATS): California State University, Sacramento (Sacramento State University)
Academic Talent Search
California State University, Sacramento
6000 J Street
Sacramento, CA 95819
Phone: 916-278-7032
E-mail: ats@csus.edu
http://edweb.csus.edu/projects/ats

Academic Talent Search (ATS): University of California, Irvine
Academic Talent Search
204 Administration Building
University of California
Irvine, CA 92697-1075
Phone: 949-824-5822; 949-824-7846
E-mail: snowdk@uci.edu
http://www.admissions.uci.edu/ats

Belin-Blank Center (B-BC): The University of Iowa
Belin-Blank Center
The University of Iowa
600 Blank Honors Center
Iowa City, IA 52242
Phone: 319-335-6148; 800-336-6463
E-mail: belinblank@uiowa.edu
http://www.education.uiowa.edu/belinblank

Carnegie Mellon Institute for Talented Elementary and Secondary Students (C-MITES): Carnegie Mellon University
C-MITES
Carnegie Mellon University
5136 Margaret Morrison St. MMP30
Pittsburgh, PA 15213

Phone: 412-268-1629
E-mail: cmites@cmu.edu
http://www.cmu.edu/cmites

Center for Talent Development (CTD):
Northwestern University
Center for Talent Development
617 Dartmouth Place
Evanston, IL 60208
Phone: 847-491-3782
E-mail: ctd@northwestern.edu
http://www.ctd.northwestern.edu

Center for Talented Youth (CTY): Johns Hopkins University
Center for Talented Youth
McAuley Hall
5801 Smith Ave., Ste. 400
Baltimore, MD 21209
Phone: 410-735-4100
E-mail: ctyinfo@jhu.edu
http://www.cty.jhu.edu

Robinson Center for Young Scholars (Washington Search
for Young Scholars—WSYS): University of Washington
Robinson Center for Young Scholars
University of Washington
Guthrie Annex 2
Box 351630
Seattle, WA 98195-1630
Phone: 206-543-4160
E-mail: cscy@u.washington.edu
http://depts.washington.edu/cscy/programs/wsys

Rocky Mountain Talent Search (RMTS): University of Denver
College of Education
Office of Academic Youth Programs
1981 S. University Blvd.
Denver, CO 80208
Phone: 303-871-2983
E-mail: rmts-info@du.edu
http://www.du.edu/education/ces/rmts.html

Talent Identification Program (TIP): Duke University
Talent Identification Program
Duke University
1121 West Main Street
Durham, NC 27701-2028
Phone: 919-668-9100
E-mail: tip@duke.edu
http://www.tip.duke.edu

Wisconsin Center for Academically Talented Youth (WCATY)
Wisconsin Center for Academically Talented Youth
2909 Landmark Place
Madison, WI 53713
Phone: 608-271-1617
E-mail: info@wcaty.org
http://www.wcaty.org

About the Author

Drawing on her experience working as a coordinator of gifted students in the National Academy of Arts, Sciences, and Engineering (NAASE), an early college entrance program at The University of Iowa, Dr. Michelle C. Muratori has been inspired to study the academic, social, and personal adjustment of students who enter college early. This research has earned her recognition from the Iowa Talented and Gifted Association, the National Association for Gifted Children, and the Mensa Education and Research Foundation and Mensa International, Ltd. She continues to advocate for and work with highly gifted students through the Center for Talented Youth at Johns Hopkins University as a senior counselor and researcher. In addition, she is a faculty associate in the Counseling and Human Services Department in the School of Professional Studies in Business and Education at Johns Hopkins University.

Printed in the United States
by Baker & Taylor Publisher Services